How to Walk With Your Hands In Your Pockets

Paint Me Green And Call Me Fern...

or

How to Walk With Your Hands In Your Pockets

collected columns by

GEORGE HESSELBERG

from the

Wisconsin State Journal, 1981-1990

with illustrations by

John Kovalic

HOT APPLE PRESS
Madison, Wisconsin

Published by
Hot Apple Press
P.O. Box 5083, Madison, Wisconsin 53705

ISBN 0-9628641-0-2

Manufactured in the United States of America
March 1991

Cover photo by Joseph W. Jackson III

For Else, Espen and Eivind.

Introduction

You're busy. I'm busy. What a day. Take a break. Here's an introduction for this book. Not all my columns are in here. Some were clunkers and some were just too tied to events to live beyond the day they were printed. I don't mind that. Someone wrote once that newspaper columnists make sculptures in the snow, and snow melts. Well, here are some of my sculptures, crooked ears and all. Please read a few at a time, put the book down and pick it up again later. I thank the people who talked to me and some of those who didn't. I thank Paul Johnson the copy editor who writes terrific headlines and knows all of the rules and loopholes. I'd like to thank all the people who said this couldn't be done, because they are the ones to blame that I did it.

Det er ingen som setter pris paa oss kranglefanter.

Real Life

Wake for the Huber Brewing Co.

My friend Jole and I attended a wake for the Huber Brewing Company last Saturday night.

It was a small crowd, just Jole and me and our wives, Else and Frankie. We had brats steamed in beer (Huber), and after dinner there was the rest of the case of Huber for us and a video ("Short Circuit") in the basement for the kids.

Huber, a product brewed in Monroe along with Augsburger, another great beer, is in danger of folding, thanks to the sellout by a couple of short-time owners. The brewery will close and the Augsburger label is being sold to Stroh. There is a chance someone will buy the brewery and keep brewing Huber in Monroe, but no one has shown the color of any money on that yet.

There was a time when I would appreciate beer not for its taste but for its cost and availability. All through college it was Huber and Leinie's, and sometimes Black Label, and never Rhinelander. In beer Hell, they serve Rhinelander, with Blatz chasers.

These days, Leinie's is part of the Miller beer family, but it is still brewed and bottled in Wisconsin, so it is still on my beerlist. I don't drink much Huber, prefer Augsburger and on payday I buy a six-pack of Capital Gartenbrau. My beer tastes are mostly local.

Jole and I, in the midst of the wake, started putting together some circumstantial evidence of the doom of Augsburger, accumulated over the past three or four years of Friday night fish fries.

First, a couple of years ago, while eating fish at a now-closed restaurant outside of Mount Horeb, we asked for a pitcher of Augsburger. (We find it convenient on a Friday night, gathered with the kids and kin, to drink beer and eat fish. If the Festival of the Lakes wants to increase attendance, it should have a family fish fry.) Anyway, over the organ music—this was a classy place—the waitress said they no longer had Augsburger on tap. It was hard to get it delivered regularly, she said.

Our eyebrows arched at the time, I recall. Hard to get? Augsburger? Right here outside of Mount Horeb, with Monroe less than a buck's worth of gas away?

Then one recent evening we were at a fish fry in New Glarus.

"We don't have Augsburger on tap anymore," the waitress said.

That one really bothered us. New Glarus is in the same phone book as Monroe. A car could run out of gas coming out of Monroe and coast to New Glarus. Whmgf, we asked between bites, mf grfng nff?

After swallowing, we asked again, what is going on?

It turned out the lack of tap Augsburger in New Glarus was a temporary glitch that had to do with attracting flies to the balcony. The lack of tap beer would soon be remedied, a bar manager told me last week, adding only half-jokingly, "if they still brew it."

But we didn't let that fact ruin our theory.

We decided that marketing success has cost Wisconsin a good beer. (Jole sometimes blames all mediocrity on marketing success, but that is another story.) Before Huber Brewing decided to make Augsburger a nationwide success, Augsburger was easy to find and moderately priced. Now there is Augsburger light and Augsburger dark and the label is all jazzed up—they don't call regular Augsburger "Augsburger" anymore, it's "Augsburger Gold"—and maybe it has marketed itself out of the local Friday night fish fry crowd.

The marketing success of Augsburger, if such a result can be called a success, might be a topic for the professionals.

Augsburger is going big time. it may be sold in all the larger airports for $4 a bottle, but you won't find it on tap at the local fish fry place.

Somewhere, probably after drinking a light beer, a marketing consultant burped, and a city lost a brewery.

■ **September 20, 1988**

Hanging Out at O'Hare

There were eight identical metal footlockers arranged two-by-two in front of the KLM check-in station at the O'Hare Field international terminal Wednesday afternoon.

Written in big white letters on each footlocker was the name of "Bill Cole," and the address of Nairobi, Kenya.

All the footlockers had rope wrapped around them, but they looked sturdy enough to survive a trampling by an elephant or the examination of even the most careless customs officer.

Mr. Cole—or the person who was checking in the footlockers, shoving them along with his feet, as people in lines with baggage tend to do—looked to be a man of about 50, short and trim.

I watched Mr. Cole, or at least the man who was pushing Mr. Cole's baggage, for a short time while cooling my heels in the terminal Wednesday. I had already spilled bright yellow mustard from a $1.50 hot dog on my red shirt and my son had spilled a $1.20 glass of orange juice on his carefully chosen green traveling outfit, so we had lost our urbane traveler look.

Hanging out at the international terminal in Chicago provides great fodder for character sketches.

What's the story behind Mr. Cole, for example. What went into the eight footlockers, and why were the sturdy metal containers bundled with rope? Can the airline's X-ray machines see into a metal footlocker? Is he carrying radio equipment for a communications outpost? Rifles, maybe, for a safari? Did his mom send along peanut butter cookies?

Or what of the stereotypical family of eight, speaking Italian, occupying a cluster of black plastic-seated chairs across from the Italian airline check-in counter? The littlest girl, about four years old, wore a frilly, floor-length dress. Several cheap suitcases were stacked round the family. Thin white string held some of the suitcases together. What are they taking back to Italy? Cowboy hats? Cheap little souvenir spoons with Lincoln's face engraved on the handle? Do they really think that kite-string will hold their suitcases together?

There was no mystery attached to the sturdy, curly gray-haired woman who approached us at the SAS check-in. It was Mrs. Nielsen, from Madison. Mrs. Nielsen has been retired for several years from her job as secretary, holding down the fort on the 11th floor of Van Hise for the UW-Madison Scandinavian Studies Department. She was taking her granddaughter to Norway for three weeks as a graduation present. She and her 21-

year-old granddaughter arrived early for SAS flight 944, which left at 5:30 p.m. Wednesday, non-stop to Oslo. They took the bus from Madison to Chicago, and so far were having a wonderful time.

Back to mysteries, what about the two short, hatless old men wearing pale-green shorts, with matching shirts? Their legs were skinny, tanned and well-muscled, and their chests fought losing battles with their shirt buttons. Except for their chests, every part of the two men appeared gnarled, even their noses. They wore socks that sagged beneath their ankle bones. Who are these two guys? Vineyard owners, perhaps? Do they play bocci together on Sunday afternoons?

Finally, there was the mid-30s-aged woman with short, curly brown hair. She was wearing a large T-shirt that featured an illustration of a panda, cuddled next to a baby panda. The woman looked to be about seven months pregnant. The stroller next to her was temporarily occupied by a large blue, bulging carry-on bag.

In the bag, along with a sweater, change of clothes and assorted toiletries, was a box of animal crackers, clearly meant for emergency appeasement of the little boy, age about two-and-a-half, who was squirming next to her, intently squashing a plastic bag filled with sweet, green seedless grapes.

The little boy was wearing a Brewers cap, with the brim pulled way down to his eyelashes.

He had on a pair of new tennis shoes purchased just for this trip, which was to be a five-week visit to his grandma and grandpa, Mor-mor and Mor-far, in southern Norway.

The mother and the little boy, before they left for the airport, placed a little bag in the spare room at home, for the father to open alone today, Father's Day.

The gift will be unwrapped while the father does the laundry, trying to get the bright yellow mustard stains out of his red shirt.

■ **June 15, 1986**

Exercise Plan Goes Belly Up

oday is the first day of spring, and a middle-aged man's thoughts turn to his bulging tummy and his unflashy 1984 Toyota Corolla, two possessions he once vowed he would never own or maintain, especially in the springtime.

I blame part of it—the stomach, that is—on a boomerang.

This was to be the winter I returned to lithedom.

The plan was to hit the exercise bicycle every night after everyone was safely—and safety is a factor when I am on the exercise bicycle—in bed. And the plan was to play pickup basketball on Sundays with the Over The Hill Gang from the office.

The result would be a sculpted torso.

Nothing breathtaking, but something that would allow me to catch an occasional glimpse of my toes, all 10 of them. (At least I think there are 10 of them.)

Something that would let me dispense with that tough decision I make every morning: whether to hitch my belt below or above my waist.

The exercise bicycle plan was the first to go awry. It is too easy to do something else, put the kids to bed, read a good mystery book.

And the basketball plan?

Last fall we went to an ice show at the Coliseum. It was boring stuff until intermission, when teen-age hawkers came on to the ice and started throwing around rings of orange plastic.

The rings were called "Wheezers," cost $5 each and were round boomerangs. These hawkers threw the rings into the crowd—did I mention they glowed in the dark?—and the rings came right back.

The Wheezers were only available in the hall, and I was not the only bored dad to pry a five-spot from his wallet, saying what fun this would be for the boys and thinking "even I can throw that."

The next day, a Saturday, I took the boys to the back yard, gave the instructions a swift read-through, grabbed the Wheezer just so, pulled back my arm and let go with a toss that surely would have spanned a major league outfield.

I'm not sure if it did or not, because I was left holding my shoulder, which felt like a barbed tongue was trying to lick its way out from my socket.

I played basketball once over the winter, and my shoulder would not even allow a set shot from the free-throw line. As we are the type of players to whom passing is a practice confined to the interstate and defense is for people who pass, I didn't have much fun.

Finally, last month I was sent to a physical therapist who explained my injury, called me mister and performed a routine of searing moist heat followed by soothing ultrasound.

He politely kept a straight face when he said I was his first boomerang injury.

So no basketball, no exercise bicycle, no lithe middle-aged man prowling the waist-32 racks at Sears, looking for something pleatless for spring.

The shoulder is almost back to pre-Wheezer condition.

I haven't gone back to the exercise bicycle. I'll take long walks after dark, the way overweight people get into shape, listening to an oldies radio station, boogalooing to an audience of one, hoping to level the knoll by the time the real spring rolls around. It's cheaper than buying a new car.   ■ **March 20, 1990**

It's Hard to Believe, But . . .

This cannot be.

I got a letter from M. Russell Hamelin, who lives at 302 Walnut St. His letter got me started on this short collection of unbelievable happenings, the sort of stuff that is just too odd to have been made up.

In Hamelin's case, he asks in his letter: "How would you like to come to your car in the garage some morning and find the entire left side missing?"

I wouldn't, but go on . . .

"That is what happened to me last Friday at 6 a.m. (This would have been mid-February) Some professional mechanic had been in the garage between midnight and 6 a.m. and taken off the left front door and the two bucket front seats and carted them off. Not a single mark or scratch on the car, not a footprint in the snow, not a tire mark. A perfectly clean job," wrote Hamelin.

The car, he added, is a 1974 Chevrolet Camaro, forest green.

He bought it new. It has 26,000 miles on it and, he said, "I'm just sick about it."

Hard to believe?

How about this "reader exchange" advertisement in the March issue of *Astronomy Magazine*:

"WANTED—Space memorabilia collector is seeking to obtain a piece of the space shuttle Challenger. Will pay or trade. Contact .... Colorado Springs, CO."

Wow, here is a guy who wants a piece of the Challenger, which exploded after takeoff in 1986.

I tried to call him, but the fellow's telephone number was unlisted.

Tracy Staedter, editorial secretary for *Astronomy Magazine*, which is based in Waukesha, said the ad was the first of its kind she has seen in the magazine. She said the magazine had received one letter critical of the ad.

Hard to believe, also, is the set of statistics on page 51 of the *Annual Report of the Postmaster General, Fiscal Year 1989.* (See? I'll read anything.)

On that page of operating statistics, are the numbers from 1986 through 1989 for different types of mail, the number of pieces mailed, the weight and the revenue.

Among the types listed is "Free for the Blind," which is mail sent for the blind as a free service.

The totals in 1987 were 41,187,000 pieces of mail, weighing 41,999,000 pounds.

The totals for 1989 dropped to 26,728,000 pieces weighing 18,463,000 pounds. Not only had the number dropped 33 percent, but the weight had dropped more than 50 percent.

After eight calls to the U.S. Postal Service in Washington, no one was able to provide a reason for this drop.

Not even the very friendly Reanne Grans of the state's office of Blind and Visually Impaired Services could explain the drop.

Nor could the equally friendly Nancy Bruckner, of the Milwaukee Library for the Blind, which is the state's clearinghouse and biggest mailer of materials to the blind. The weight of material sent has gone down, she acknowledged, and possibly there are fewer items being produced for the blind, but neither of those factors would explain a drop of millions in the number of pieces mailed.

And finally, in the unbelievable genre, came a telephone call from Ed McGrath of Oregon.

One day last month his wife, Lisa, was writing out checks to pay bills, including a bill for $175.96 for the monthly car-loan payment to Chrysler Credit and a bill for $66 for a student loan payment.

Absent-mindedly, she sent both checks in the envelope to the student loan collection office at the Great Lakes Higher Education Corporation.

A couple of weeks later, the McGraths got a letter from Chrysler, wondering what happened to their car payment.

We paid it, said McGrath, puzzled, since he had the canceled check in hand.

Closer inspection showed the check had been made out to Chrysler Credit but cashed by the student loan outfit. Valley Bank, which holds the account, agreed to un-cash the check, but only for a fee.

McGrath thought it odd that the student loan people would cash a check made out to Chrysler ("Hey, I can't cash a check made out to my brother, can I?" he asked.) But he was told by the student loan people it was the McGraths' fault, since they sent the check.

And the strangest part, he said, is that the usual student loan payment is only $66, but the check was for $175.96.

If it had been the other way around, if he had sent a check for $66 when he owed $175, they might have paid attention to the "Pay to the order of . . ."

The bank, by the way, told him he would have to pay a fee for un-cashing the check, but so far he has not been billed for it.

■ **March 4, 1990**

Success Measured by Odd Rule

Well, paint me green and call me Fern, state government just keeps getting curiouser and curiouser.

Among other oddities, we now have, courtesy of His Humbleness, Gov. Tommy Thompson, a new definition of "tremendously successful."

Thompson was complaining recently about the failure of the Legislature to expand a state workfare program, known as WEJT, for Work Experience and Job Training.

"This program is tremendously successful in getting people off welfare and a broad-based WEJT expansion initiative should be included in the bill," said His Politicalness.

The WEJT is a noble project, but not even a whole roomful of political truth-stretchers could accurately describe it as "tremendously successful." Only a charitable reading of an April 1989 audit of the program would even bring it near the word "successful." The audit, in fact, said the program results are "mixed."

How mixed?

■ The program Thompson called "tremendously successful" was so chaotic in one county, Kenosha, it was nearly scrapped altogether.

■ The "tremendously successful" program had inadequate cost information, poor state leadership, conflicting descriptions of goals and inadequate or missing data required to discover if clients even got jobs—a result, of course, that was a major purpose of the entire program.

■ The "tremendously successful" program in calendar year 1988 allocated $886,000 in 13 counties for "post AFDC" day care, a necessary aid to help welfare mothers stay on jobs. How much did those 13 counties spend of that $886,000? Only 1 percent, or $9,003.

This goes on and on. The point is that the program is young, needs work, and administrators promise changes. The day-care money, for example, is now being used. But the program certainly is not "tremendously successful," and saying it causes more harm than good.

■   ■   ■

I, for one, am glad someone finally discovered that the sexual revolution of the 1969s (woops, 1960s) and 1970s, didn't happen.

Having based a portion of my life on a thorough study of certain black-light posters popular in 1969-70, I was still waiting for, er, it to appear.

Twenty years ago, I was pretty sure the sexual revolution would arrive braless at my dormitory room door wearing a peasant dress and carrying the answers to my astronomy test.

Never happened, of course.

More than one kid went through adolescence and early manhood with the same unopened condom package imprinting a circle on his wallet.

This past week, sex researchers in Indiana (or air-conditioning experts in the Arctic) released a book based on surveys of a decade ago proving, they say, that the sexual revolution never happened.

Well, maybe it did and maybe it didn't.

What these fellows always forget, when chronicling revolutions of the past, is that there may have been a lot of peasants storming the castle, but just as many or more were still at home milking the cows.

Which reminds me of a short conversation I had Monday morning while standing in a dusty La Crosse County farmyard. Espen and Eivind—my two sons, ages five and almost three— had just alighted from a long ride in an old horse wagon, providing ballast while my friend Dan Jones exercised his Clydesdale horses.

There in the barnyard stood a little boy, barefoot, in shorts and a T-shirt.

His name was Chad Jerome, age four.

Chad came up to us to talk about dogs, and just as the chat got into the Voofing stage, a brown van pulled into the yard.

Chad—age four, remember—looked at the van and said: "Here comes the vet; we must be breedin' cows today."

■ July 6, 1989

This Poker Club Doesn't Cut a Deal

*T*here is a group in Madison that meets for poker whenever a basement or deck can be commandeered and when the pocket change starts to overflow the dresser.

The rules are simple (I have heard.) Only three bet raises allowed, $5 pot limit, quarter maximum bet. Bring your own beer, the cheaper the better. Host supplies the cheese and crackers.

Also, a card laid is a card played. If you sneak a look you fold your hand and you match the pot.

Over the years, the group has had its share of odd happenings (I have heard). A tablecloth was set on fire one night and once a Yupster was nearly beheaded by an errant Asti Spumanti cork. I could go on, but the point here is there is a hard and fast rule that the best cards win the pot.

Not the second best cards.

Winner take all, even if "all" is only a few bucks in nickels and quarters.

Naturally, the OHNLTBW club was interested when a Madison fellow won the World Series of Poker.

Phil Hellmuth Jr., 24, won the series a couple of weeks ago at Binion's Horseshoe Casino. The winner of that series was supposed to get $755,000 and the runner-up $302,000.

Now comes the New York *Village Voice* sports column, "Jockbeat," to fill in the blanks behind that poker victory. The column this week said Hellmuth, with the best hand showing but before the final cards were revealed, proposed a deal to his competitor, previous poker champion and fellow "poker brat packer" Johnny Chan.

"In return for locking in a split before the rest of the hand was dealt out, Hellmuth would sweeten Chan's cut of the total prize money. That way, if a freaky turn of the cards gave Chan the hand and he went on to win the tournament, Hellmuth's chunk of the loot would still be guaranteed, probably at around $655,000."

That is known as hedging a bet.

The *Voice,* with no attribution, said the two players got up and left the table, mid-hand, to discuss this. The *Voice* hedges its own column by not saying if there really was a deal or not. It ended with the note that "as the two big-time gamblers had already ensured, to the loser goes at least part of the spoils."

This was true anyway, since the runner-up was supposed to get $302,000, without any deal cut.

The column noted that "deal-cutting like this happens all the time in major tournaments, but no observer could recall it happening in the middle of a hand at the putative world championship."

The two were playing a no-limit Texas Hold'em poker game, in which the players can use two cards in their hands combined with three cards on the table to make the best poker hand.

Hellmuth in this game held a pair of nines (showing) and Chan had an ace and a seven. The two players shared a pair of kings in the open. So, in the end, Hellmuth's two pair beat Chan's one pair. All of the wire services said he won $755,000; he did not deny it; and he took a private jet back to Madison amidst hoopla and huzzahs.

I wanted to know if Hellmuth cut a deal, a concept of poker new to me and certainly to fellow members of the OHNLTBW club. Tracking down a big-time poker player is not very difficult. He returned my call within an hour and I asked him about the "deal."

He hadn't seen the column, but said there was no deal cut with Chan.

"We didn't make a deal. We went outside to talk about a deal, but we didn't make one. We made no deal, and then came back and played," said Hellmuth.

In a poker tournament, once the game is down to the final three or four players, it is not unusual for the players to make a deal about splitting the final pots, said Hellmuth.

He is known in professional poker circles, though, for not cutting deals.

"I'm an exception to the rule. I like to walk away with 100 percent of the money," he said, adding that he understands the need to make deals because of high expenses involved in staying on the poker tour.

Hellmuth, who is single, learned to play poker in the UW-Madison Memorial Union.

He said a couple of years ago he might have called himself a "compulsive gambler," but he doesn't gamble any more.

"I played craps, baccarat, blackjack and I got killed," he said.

"Now I only play poker."

Poker is not gambling?

"It's mostly a game of skill, like golf," he said.

That's what the members of the One High, None Low, Two Both Ways club have been telling their spouses for years.

Unfortunately, considering the combined poker acumen of the club members, it is difficult to say that with a straight face.

■ **June 4, 1989**

Homeowner with a Recalcitrant Lawn

1 I remember as if it were 10 minutes instead of three years ago, standing in front of the house we eventually bought, telling the eager-to-please owner "the lawn doesn't make that much difference to me."

Not to worry, I said. The status, condition and growth of vegetation on my property are the least of my concerns.

So why am I upset that a golf ball, dropped from a height of three feet on to my back yard, will bounce up four feet?

Those front page photographs of farmers spraying herbicide on dusty fields do not tell the sad drought story of the homeowner with a concrete lawn.

My lawn, which this spring has been fed, wed, raked and watered, responded by turning into a surface you can draw chalk pictures on. It crunches like corn flakes when I walk on it.

I have stopped asking for advice from my colleagues. My

lawn now joins my driveway as an embarrassment to suburbia.

My lawn looks like someone slept on it funny.

I may put a stocking over my telephone receiver and call the gardener's hotline. Here are some of my questions: Could it be that I have been trying to make a fairway out of a no-way?

Is there a type of lush green grass that turns rock and clay into sponge?

Why don't moles eat dandelions? Do they carry maps drawn on graph paper, with a little "X" by the new sod?

How come the grass turned brown over my septic tank?

Why does the cover of the grill leave a brown circle mark on the grass?

Why can't I get grass to grow on a hillside?

Why are my hickory trees dying?

Who took the cover off my big plastic bucket of bird seed, causing a gray squirrel convention in my backyard for six hours? When we broke up the party, I swear some were wearing leaves like little lampshades on their heads, singing, "We're in the millet, we're in the millet."

Who ate the middles—not the tops or the roots—off my marigolds?

Why are my chives bigger than my lilacs?

Are chives and parsley incompatible? Is it winner-take-all when they are planted next to each other?

Why can't I get grass to grow anywhere but inside the sandbox?

Has anyone else considered tying the handles together on the lawnmower so that it will keep running when you let go of it? Do you feel guilty about it? Can you be arrested for it? Is beer good for a lawn?

I know my lawn is always good for a beer. ■ **May 26, 1988**

Lessons From Life and Lotteries

I won the lottery once.

When I was working as a night watchman for the Norwegian Telepone Company in Oslo, I spent 10 kroner for a ticket and won 50 kroner in the monthly Norwegian lottery.

My reaction to the win was to invest the 50 kroner, which was less than $10, into five 10-kroner lottery tickets the next month.

At the time, I was working for the telephone company and as a bartender in an Italian restaurant in Oslo, and taking classes at the University of Oslo. I was living in a one-room fifth-floor walkup on Sigurdsgate, around the corner from the Munch Museum.

Nearly every kroner I earned went to pay the rent and to buy cigarette papers and rolling tobacco. Booze I bought tax-free cheap from an embassy guard, and I ate leftover pizza at the restaurant. I bought a monthly bus and trolley pass. I read magazines for free at the embassy library and I ate the same type of lunch every day: open-faced sandwiches, brown cheese on whole wheat bread, with two fat slices of cucumber on top.

I had friends in more or less the same financial boat as I was, and we would have dinners where everyone brought one ingredient for the stew. We would cook the stew and drink government-bottled red wine and talk all night about politics, sex, literature, fights with the immigration office, rent, ways to get cheap train tickets and jobs on freighters. We would talk about who finally gave up and went back home and who would be next. We would talk trash about the short-timers. We would talk about what a truly great life we had, or would have if we had only finished the novel, married into a shipping family, or figured out how to skim the profits from a restaurant that employed only foreign workers.

I lived in an unfurnished room, with kitchen privileges. With help from the telephone company janitor, I made a comfortable bed out of a piece of foam and scrap lumber I took from the telephone company trash pile and brought back to my room piece by piece on the bus.

I kept detailed, daily accounts of how much money I made, how much I spent and what I spent it on.

I walked long distances in the old parts of town to look at window displays and old buildings.

Everything I did was based on when my paychecks arrived. (There's something that hasn't changed.) But then I won 50 kroner in that damned lottery.

This, it seemed, was a way of making money that I could live with.

I had quadrupled my investment, from 10 kroner to 50 kroner, in three weeks.

That 50 kroner the next month should then return 250 kroner, and the next month, 1,250 kroner. In six months time, I would be up to 6,250 kroner a month, or about $1,000, with no end in sight. I would be making so much money I would eat at restaurants twice a month, maybe even buy meat for my open-faced sandwiches.

There was nothing logical or rational about the way I planned this.

As the song goes, when you got nothing, you got nothing to lose.

Unfortunately, in the lottery business, it costs money to dream.

I played the lottery monthly until I left the country in September 1976, usually buying five tickets at 10 kroner each. While I scrounged for bread and cheese, I dropped 1,000 kroner on lottery tickets. I never won again, but I still buy a couple of tickets whenever I go back to Norway to visit friends and relatives.

There are those who say that a lottery in Wisconsin is a good thing.

I'd say a lottery is a good thing if you get a job working for it.

Using my limited knowledge, I would say a lottery is a good way to get the poor to invest their money in something that makes pretty thin soup.　　　　　　　　■ **May 22, 1988**

All's Well Under Starry Skies at the Silver Screen

The vans line up in the back row, a gesture of courtesy that all the passengers in compact cars parked in front of them remark upon with appreciation.

Kids wearing Snoopy and ET pajamas and fluffy pink bedroom slippers bound about the rows of parked cars as daylight fades.

A football floats in a wobbly arc in front of the large screen.

This is the drive-in, the Badger Fourplex, and the show that is just beginning has nothing to do with the Ghostbusters, which won't start until dusk.

Begin by checking out the neighbors in the lot. A station wagon to the right, a station wagon to the left. It's Kid City, but the parents seem to be in control even though the Old Man is dozing, tummy up against the wheel and Mother is keeping an eye out for spills and bumps and an ear out for impractical requests and minor sibling disturbances.

In front, a compact car which, as they used to say in high school, looks like it requires two people to drive, since two people are sitting behind the steering wheel.

Time for the promenade.

Unbuckle the tyke, hoist him up on the shoulders and join the people strolling through lanes of pickup trucks parked backwards with mattresses and pillows in the back. Past dinosaur cars with children already sitting on the blanket-covered roofs. Past the lawn-chair and boom-box crowd, a byproduct of the wonderful idea to put the movie sound on the AM radio instead of through speakers you hang on to the window.

People on dates head for the concession stand and return with buckets of popcorn.

People with children unfold the brown paper shopping bags, already greasy at the bottom, filled with still warm popcorn.

Parents herd their children to the bathrooms.

Late arrivals prowl the lanes looking for the few unfilled spots. Compacts have the edge, sometimes squeezing in door handle to door handle. No fear, there is an escape route through the hatchback.

It's still daylight and the neckers are hard at it with their

PDAs (Public Displays of Affection), bucket seats or not.

Later, torn between watching the movie and taking the next step after Meaningful Glance, there may be an argument. There are clues: accidental leaning on the horn, the brake lights suddenly going off and on, the sound of a car door slamming.

The not-so-acquainted on their first or second date by now have edged a little closer, having used up their Bill Murray-Caddyshack routine. First moves, casual, calculated, are being made.

The radio is switched to 6.4. The windows are rolled up against the mosquitoes and the station wagon conversations.

Darkness brings privacy.

The kid is asleep in the back.

Mother is asleep in the front.

The Old Man pops a beer and tears the sides of the paper bag so he doesn't make so much noise grabbing for the popcorn.

"This," he sighs, "is the life." ■ **July 8, 1984**

'I Was There' Sounds Like a Fish Story

The launching of the Hubble telescope gives me a chance to air a longstanding observation.

That is, in 10 years, do you think there will be an astronomer or physicist in the country who will say he or she did NOT work on the Hubble telescope?

What I mean is, will the Hubble be to astronomers what Woodstock is to hippies?

Perhaps you've overheard the conversation: "Great concert, sort of like a rock fest, huh?"

"Yeah, a little like Woodstock."

"Woodstock? You were there?"

"Sure, and lemme tell you that movie was nothing like it really happened."

Well, these days, who of the tender ages 38-44 was not at Woodstock?

Just as everyone who ever lived in Chicago in the 1930s claims to have been at Wrigley Field in 1932 when Babe Ruth called his shot, and everyone who lives in New York was at the Polo Grounds on Oct. 3, 1951, when Bobby Thompson hit the "shot heard round the world," a three-run ninth-inning home run to clinch the pennant for the Giants.

And every Midwestern Catholic was on hand for the pope's 1979 visit to Iowa.

Is there a football fan in Wisconsin who did NOT see the "ice bowl" plunge of Bart Starr to the end zone?

And how many people have told you lately that they personally know someone who won the lottery, or who discarded a winning lottery ticket, or who always picked a certain number but one week forgot to buy a ticket and THAT number won?

How many hard-eyed reporters have claimed to be "the last reporter out" before the fall of Saigon.

And this: Last month, for the 20th anniversary of Earth Day, I ran across mention of at least two people who were anointed "father" of Earth Day. (This is not counting Gaylord Nelson, who is now known as the "grandfather" of Earth Day.) And if you read the obituaries, every once in a while someone's obit will note that he or she "worked on the Manhattan project." One recent obit noted the deceased's claim to fame was that he worked on security for the Manhattan project.

Everything gets exaggerated with the retelling.

Someone saw it on television or read about it and then repeated the story to someone else, who told a friend, saying he knows a friend who was there, and on it goes.

Or the event was so big (Woodstock, Hubble) that to be part of it was only natural (and almost impossible to confirm), and not to have been part of it leaves a gap in the credentials.

I'll bet when that gospel group got together at Bethsaida, the five barley loaves and two small fishes that were available for brunch fed a dozen or so, and they stretched it with an okra salad, followed by a business meeting, a speaker and gospel singing.

Imagine the conversations on the 20th anniversary of the Loaves and Fish Concert: "Yeah, I was at Bethsaida, what a trip."

"I heard people were eating their sandals."

"No, the Man was there, he took care of it."

"How many did he feed?"

"I think it was 5,000, not including the begotten."

"Wow, were you there for the, what's the name of that group?"

"Temptations? Yeah, but the sound system was awful."

"Rowdy?"

"Are you kidding? They say John threw the first stone."

"No? Say, Matthew, did you have a good seat?"

"Hey, I was on the stage crew."   ■ **May 8, 1990**

Selling TVs From the Trunk of a Car

This is a story about why you shouldn't try to sell stolen television sets from a car trunk at 11 on a Wednesday night on North Baldwin Street.

Two guys meet at a tavern. One a resident of Madison, the other a stranger. They do what guys do at a tavern. They drink, they shoot pool, they even talk. They go to the Madison guy's home to drink and watch Playboy videos. After an argument, the visitor leaves.

The next day, while at work, the Madison guy gets a call that his home has been burglarized and two video recorders and a television set are missing.

The guy gets a funny feeling he knows who did it, so on his way home from work he cruises, looking for the car of the guy who came to his house the night before.

He passes by Baldwin Steet and sees the headlights and front end of an old Ford. He circles the block, sees the guy with a bunch of men standing around looking at something in the back seat of the car, beneath a blanket. The Midnight Appliance Store was open for business.

He drives back to East Washington Avenue and flags down Police Officer Sandy Theune. Theune drives over, asks a few questions and the suspect identifies himself with a car title as Herman C. Scharrer, 54.

The suspected stolen television and video recorders were

among other items on display.

So a perpetrator is apprehended.

Police explain he is under arrest, and the stranger's reaction is to suddenly say he has a heart condition and, according to police reports, to complain "that he is feeling some chest pain and numbness in his left arm." He "began to breathe in a shallow manner."

It doesn't take a grant-writing expert to know what may be going on here. A miracle in reverse. What was well and on the way to jail is now sick and on the way to the hospital.

At the hospital, the clerk dutifully asks Mr. Herman C. Scharrer if he has ever been there before.

He says no. The hospital computer responds that Scharrer was admitted in 1982, when he lived in Mount Horeb.

Scharrer (the burglary suspect) says he has never been in Mount Horeb.

Several officers are now in on the case, hoping to identify the suspect. The next day, detective George Croal joins the hunt. Police have the car title used for identification, but no address or telephone for Scharrer. A description of Scharrer, though, says he has brown eyes. The suspect has blue eyes.

After dozens of telephone calls, the Anoka, Minn., police department reports they picked up Scharrer for drunken driving a month ago. More phone calls. The man in the hospital says he has never been to Mount Horeb, but Herman C. Scharrer used to work in Mount Horeb. A real Mount Horebonian, who knows Scharrer, is brought in. That's not him, says the Horebonian.

Finally, Croal gets a set of fingerprints from the burglary suspect-aka-Scharrer. He calls Neil Purtell, longtime Madison FBI agent, who sends a copy of the prints by telephone line to the FBI fingerprint lab in Washington, D.C.

The fingerprint technician in Washington looks at the prints. A colleague, Terry Auburgey, walks over, looks at the prints and says "Hey, I know who that is."

Auburgey, it turns out, had just processed a set of prints identical to the ones sent along by Croal. They belong to Henry Bob Martin, 48, wanted for escape on a parole violation from Santa Fe, N.M.

So Scharrer is really Martin, who is suspected of stealing the Madison guy's stuff.

Talk about making your own luck: the guy bothering to drive around looking for the suspect, then the chance of finding a cop on East Washington Avenue exactly when you need one, then the tell-tale computer message about the ersatz Scharrer's earlier hospitalizaion, the Minnesota connection, Croal going the extra mile to touch base with the feds, the fingerprint technician being curious enough to wonder what a colleague is up to.

The real Scharrer?

He's working in Minneapolis, living with his sister, Croal said, unaware of all the fuss. ■ **April 21, 1988**

Relighting the Limelight For a Hero

 ome heroes stick around to bask in the fleeting limelight. Others just climb back aboard the merry-go-round without so much as a glance over the shoulder, and no one calls them back for an ovation.

So it was with Lee Jaromin, a young man from Tomah who slipped in and out of the news last week with nothing more than temporary local acclaim.

Jaromin is a distributor/salesman for Cap's Distributing, a Tomah company. It is his job to drive around to towns in southwestern Wisconsin selling candy and other foods to businesses.

A week ago Wednesday at about noon, he was on the job, driving south on Highway Z in Adams County in the town of Strongs Prairie, which is near the Wisconsin River.

A few minutes before Jaromin drove by, George and Harriet Kennedy of rural Friendship were driving on Highway Z, northbound, in their 1987 Cutlass, on the way to Friendship for a senior citizen bowling outing.

As they approached the bridge, the car slid out of control and down a hill, headed toward the Castle Rock Wisconsin River backwater.

"We thought we were going to stop before we got to the water, but the car just kept going faster and faster," said Harriet, 74.

The car was in open, cold water, about 20 yards from the icy shore.

George, 79, a retired Chicago firefighter and a strong swimmer, crawled out the window first.

"He had his heavy fleece jacket on and he thought he could reach bottom, but he went right down and his cap came floating up. It's funny now but it wasn't funny then," Harriet remembered.

George started swimming and was halfway to shore when the current started pulling.

That is about the time Jaromin drove over the bridge, saw a truck with other rescuers stopped, so he stopped, too.

"I saw the car was partially submerged and Harriet was still in it and George was in the water," he said.

"I yelled for George to come to shore, he was apparently in shock and he went under once. I figured he wasn't going to make it so I jumped in and swam out about 20 feet or so and helped him up; he was incoherent," Jaromin said. He noted another fellow helped pull George up.

"It was deeper than I thought. I'm 6-foot-3 and it was over my head."

The car's front end was now beginning to submerge and Harriet was still in the car, so Jaromin jumped into his car and drove to a small gas station-store to call for help.

"When I came back, the car was submerged and she was sort of standing on it. I jumped in again and tried to go get her," he said.

But then, Jaromin said, "I cramped up, I couldn't make it."

By this time, he had jumped into the icy backwater twice, and Harriet was up to her waist in water, standing on the car.

Someone found a short rope, and someone else had an old boat cushion. The rope was too short, though, so Jaromin took off his belt and added that to the rope and swam out to Harriet with the rope in one hand because "the rope was so short I needed the extra six feet of stretch with my hand."

Said Harriet: "I dove in off the hood and grabbed the cushion, and this boy jumped in and pulled me out."

Actually, Jaromin said, he grabbed her and people on the shore pulled them in.

"She's a tough one," said Jaromin, admiringly, of Harriet. "She was calm, she had a big heavy jacket on but she held on pretty good."

The authorities arrived after Harriet got to shore, he said.

"I didn't stick around. I gave the police my business card and I took off for home," he said.

Soaking wet, he drove 45 miles home.

He said he had great help from two men who worked for the Wisconsin River Power Company, and a couple who provided blankets.

Jaromin, 29, is single and he has worked for Cap's for nine years. He lives in rural Tomah with his mother, Janet. She was a little upset with her boy for driving 45 miles after getting out of the river. She said he got a heckuva cold because of it.

George and Harriet Kennedy were treated for hypothermia at an Adams County hospital. "We're fine," said Harriet.

Harriet said she and her husband are thankful for Jaromin's help, and they have told him so.

"Nobody else seemed to know what to do," Harriet said.

And now, the ovation, please. ■ **February 4, 1990**

Nowhere Near The Bull's Eye

I'm sick and tired of not being "targeted."

I don't seem to be included in any of the trendy advertising campaigns, present or planned. As a target, I'm out of radar range. I'm a negative option. I've been watching television and reading magazines and newspapers. I can take a hint. I don't need a voice on a loudspeaker to say "PLEASE REMOVE YOURSELF FROM THE TARGET AREA."

So maybe I'm not a fertile single white party bimbo. They get a new cigarette. Shoot-heck, I left those target areas years ago when they stopped making Chesterfield straights, and I got married.

The more I think about it, the fewer the target areas I can remember crossing into during these, my "prime target" years.

I've been confused about target areas ever since Burger King said "Herb" was a typical Wisconsin guy. I never met anyone in Wisconsin who even remotely resembled "Herb," though I once met a guy named "Linus" who wore the same sort of clothes as the Burger King "Herb."

I am "thirtysomething" but I watch that show and don't see myself anywhere in it or any other television show in which no one ever does anything in the bathroom. The target group there appears to be witty sarcastic "creative" people who were born without kidneys and with self-cleaning hands. I'm always going to the bathroom and washing my hands, in that order, thank you.

I drink beer, but I can't see myself as a target of beer commercials that feature shapely women emerging soaking wet from fountains of youth. I look at them, sure (I'm not that far out of the target area), but my target fountain would emit six or seven lumpy fellow reporters reeking of cigar smoke and wet only under their chins. I admit it doesn't make an appetizing image, but in a group after a poker game they make a pretty good target, leaning against each other like that.

So I'm not in the target of ad campaigns that want to convince me I should become addicted to nicotine. I can live with that.

(Besides, tobacco companies have been targeting men for years and no one ever had a congressional hearing to complain specifically about that. There's a message there somewhere, and it's not comforting.)

And I'm certainly not the target of ad campaigns that want to convince me I should become obsessed with perfectly proportioned wet women and light beer.

So of what am I a target?

Unfortunately, I believe I am a target of a misfire.

As near as I can tell, if I am a target, I am a target of those corn root insecticide commercials.

I like to watch them. I wouldn't mind chumming with some of the people pictured who kneel in the cornfields and uncover deadly worms in the soil. They look like people who go to the bathroom and wash their hands. Alas, my corn roots don't need insecticide.

I might wander into other target areas once in a while, but I've never really been on the bull's-eye.

Face it. I'm a fringe target.

Sell me something. Please.   ■ **February 27, 1990**

Hilda's Prize Made His Day In Fairest Way

t is a short drive from Madison to Columbus. About 30 miles and, one day last week, 81 years.

I was on "time off," one of those use-it-or-lose-it deals where at the end of the year you realize you may have time off coming and a middle-management type walks up to your desk and says "use it or lose it."

So I was using it, and on a foggy morning I drove to Columbus.

I was looking for the Columbus Antique Mall, and it was easy enough to find. Take a right off the main street at the lights, then a left and drive until you get to the water utility and there it is about a half block on the right. Park in back and take a look at what appears to be an abandoned factory.

On the inside, it appears as if somebody's attic exploded and the contents were allowed to fall neatly onto shelves. Lots of shelves, some too close together, some filled with junk, some filled with treasure, some filled with I don't know what. The impulse is to walk around with hands in pockets, elbows close. It's the "break-it-and-buy-it" position, and I use it in close quarters.

There are antique malls popping up all over. A big old unused building is recycled into a place for antique/collectible dealers to show their wares. Every nook is filled with something a granny might have thrown out long ago, then changed her mind and hauled back to the attic again.

It's the second or third best thing to go to (behind a good farm auction and a trip to a car junkyard), on a free day.

I was simply wandering and, on this day, I was the only customer in the place. That's ideal save for the absence of anyone to ask the usual auction question of, "What the heck do you think this is?"

I saw a few things I liked but would not get into my house on a bet, such as the beautifully framed poster of all the members of the Norwegian parliament of 1905, the year Norway was relieved of the Swedish burden. As the saying goes, a collectible is not necessarily an antique, and an antique is not necessarily a collectible.

I bought a set of brass napkin rings and a few (overpriced) old Norwegian post cards from a neutral fellow who wouldn't give me the advertised 15-percent discount because none of my purchases was over $10 per item. Earlier I overheard him talking about the shoplifting problem with a woman exhibitor who was threatening to quit the mall.

Aside from the oversized mechanical Santa and some obvious junk (such as the McDonald's Happy Meal toys), and the lack of collectors to kibitz and horse-trade with, it was a pleasant stroll.

And I bought something else. Something that I was not collecting, something that I do not intend to sell again.

On the second floor of this old factory building in an untended corner exhibit was a small bookshelf that held a small book of 242 rough-edged pages bound in soft leather that was torn on the front cover. The book is embossed on the cover with the *Selected Poems of W.C. Bryant.* On the spine, the title is *Bryant's Early Poems.*

For that alone the book would have interested me only a little.

But I was drawn to the inscription inside, written with a sharp-tipped fountain pen, and dated 7/16/1909. It said, in Norwegian, "First prize for grades in the Norway Grove congregation's religious school. To Hilda Esse. From P.E. Nelson."

Norway Grove was (and still is) a small community near DeForest.

The book cost $4.50 and it is a pleasure to hold and to read.

But I wondered about Hilda Esse and what she must have thought about winning first prize in 1909 and if these poems had any meaning for her later. Or if she just thought, "Jeepers, I work my butt off in this school and all I win is a lousy book of poems."

And I wondered about a religious school in 1909 giving a little girl what might seem to some to be a daring book written by someone considered a social reformer. And the book does have a few racy pronouncements about love.

There is a nifty poem that any rural Wisconsin boy might have written, called "Oh Fairest of the Rural Maids," which Bryant wrote of his wife:

> Oh fairest of the rural maids! Thy birth was in the
> forest shades;
> Green boughs, and glimpses of the sky, were all that
> met thy infant eye.

But in this little book of poems Hilda Esse had turned over the corner of only one page, which held a portion of the love poem "A Song of Pitcairn's Island."

It is a woman speaking and she says:

> I'm glad to see my infant wear thy soft blue eyes and
> sunny hair.

Still, I was drawn back to the fairest of the rural maids, and I read it right there in the empty Columbus Antique Mall, which is why I was in a good mood when I left. How can you not be when you read of the fairest:

"Thy eyes are springs, in whose serene
"And silent waters heaven is seen."

Wow. ■ **February 18, 1990**

A Generation is a Terrible Thing to Waste

It was a spur of the moment argument, starting with someone's comment about drug abuse. The point the commentator made was that "if they can afford drugs, they can afford their own treatment. Why should the public have to pay for it."

No, let's put our money into prisons, into penalties, not treatment, the commentator said.

My response was that the public would pay a lot more if treatment or rehabilitation or education was not provided in one way or another. The public might save money by spending money, I said.

The debate lagged. I got mad and quit the argument.

But the same topic has come up again, this time with birth control and abortion-related questions.

So I have been gathering evidence.

Let's take the mother who was drunk when her baby girl was born in Milwaukee a couple of weeks ago. The baby's blood alcohol content was 0.163 at birth, and the mother's was 0.38. Drunk in this state is 0.10. The baby died five weeks after her birth.

Emphasis now has been placed on ways to punish the mother in case a similar situation arises.

I say the emphasis should be on educating the mother. What are the chances, do you suppose, that this mother had prenatal care? Or, if she did, that she recognized its importance?

There is now evidence that syphilis in newborns has soared to record levels because of women who swap sex for drugs and pass on the disease to their fetuses.

The Centers for Disease Control said 691 cases of congenital syphilis were reported in 1988, up 54 percent from the year before and the highest total since the days before penicillin, a Knight-Ridder News Service story reported.

Babies in New York City accounted for 357 of the cases in 1988, or just over half the national total.

"The practice of trading sex with multiple partners for drugs, especially cocaine [or] crack, now appears to play a major role in the transmission of syphilis," the Atlanta-based CDC concluded.

The New York study showed that only 51 percent of the mothers in the New York study reported any prenatal care visits.

Syphilis, a common sexually transmitted disease, can be treated in most cases with penicillin or other antibiotics, although it's too late to reverse birth defects in many children born with the disease.

Or how about this? A new study at Hutzel Hospital in Detroit's inner city, the most extensive in the nation to date, found that 42.7 percent of its newborn babies were exposed to drugs while in their mothers' wombs, the Chicago Tribune reported.

Dr. Ira Chasnoff, president of the Chicago-based National Association for Perinatal Addiction Research and Education, said the Detroit findings "reflect what we are seeing in places like Chicago, New York, Los Angeles, Washington and other cities with a major drug problem."

"We know these drugs cause handicaps, learning problems and other difficulties," Ostrea said. "You're talking about a generation of children who will suffer."

"We are not talking about a medical problem," Wiener said. "We are talking about a societal problem. We already know that children who get off to a bad start tend to have problems later in life. These babies have lost the battle before they were even born. If there is mental impairment or neurological damage, we are all in for a rough time."

These babies are among the saddest victims of the nation's drug habit, the Tribune reported. Their shriveled bodies, sometimes weighing no more than a pound or two, bristle with tubes and wires connected to machines that breath for them, feed them and monitor their vital signs.

The nurses who work in this Detroit hospital unit tell of nurturing these babies back to health, only to turn them over to drug-addled mothers with scant prospects of providing any sort of decent child-rearing environment, the Tribune reported.

Typical intensive-care costs for treating babies exposed to drugs range from $7,500 to $31,000, although it is not uncommon to see medical bills soar as high as $150,000. Since most of the mothers are indigent, the costs are borne by Medicaid.

Mothers of drug-affected children need intensive, follow-up training in nurturing and parenting, Chasnoff said. "What we have to do," he said, "is provide the kind of active intervention and support that can improve the outcomes for these children."

See my point? Pay now or pay later. When they start complaining about sex education, about rehabilitation costs, about prenatal care costs, consider the other costs:

The medical costs, if you want to concentrate on the bottom line.

Or the societal costs, the costs of a true lost generation.

Take some of that drug war money and put it to use to find that generation.   ■ **January 21, 1990**

Even If It's Urban Legend, It's Horrible

*T*he note said: "Welcome to the world of AIDS."

The note was the payoff, the punchline, in a story that was passed along to me by a staff member, a counselor, at a Madison high school.

She called just after Easter and told the following story:

A group of Madison high school girls traveled to Florida together for spring break. That sounds a little young, to me, but it is fairly commonplace these days.

While in Florida one of the girls had sex with a stranger, a good-looking young man. It happens.

When the two parted, he gave her a wrapped present that she was supposed to open when she got back to Madison.

She did.

The present contained a tiny coffin, and inside the coffin was a note that said "Welcome to the world of AIDS."

The girl later tested positive for the HIV virus.

This story was supposedly told to the counselor by a friend of the girl involved in the story.

She called to express her outrage that someone would purposely attempt to infect an innocent youth with acquired immune deficiency syndrome. She called it "casual murder."

I suggested that the whole story sounded like an urban legend. One of those rumors that gets repeated and repeated, but it always happens to a friend of a friend and, when tracked down, the truth disappears.

I urged the woman to discuss this with the girl again and try to track down the girl involved in the story and call me back.

She agreed, but did not call me back.

I still think it was a spring break rumor, probably passed from one group of high school travelers to another. I heard another version of the same story from a student at a different Madison high school.

But the story stuck, and, if it's true or if it's not, Earl Bricker doesn't think it's very funny or even educational in a "safe-sex" sort of way.

"I would be very surprised if that story is true," said Bricker, who is executive director of the Madison AIDS Support Network.

"But I would also be the last person to say something like this hasn't happened. Out of the [250 million] people in this country, and of those who may have AIDS or be HIV infected, at least one might be unbalanced."

He noted a similar anecdote is told in the book *And the Band Played On,* a fascinating account of the start and public exposure of the AIDS plague.

And, he remembered, a recent Broom Street Theater play included a character who "did that very thing," purposely passing along the disease.

"We objected to it because it seemed to promote that kind of occurrence," he said.

On a broader level, AIDS hoaxes and jokes make the work of AIDS support networks and agencies more difficult—if that is possible.

Part of educating the public is to convince them "to get angry about the disease, not at the people who have it," Bricker said.

"It becomes a popular perception for people who say all AIDS victims want to do is spread it," he said.

And, adds Bricker, these days, people with AIDS are victims of hoaxes, too, just like everyone else who tries to cure an incurable disease or medical condition.

"As with any disease, certain treatments are promoted. Our role is not so much to direct a person's health care, but if someone comes in and says they've read about something and they want to try it, we don't try to talk them out of it. We do try to investigate it."

No malady exists without a cure that quacks. In California last January a doctor was arrested after investigators discovered he was treating AIDS patients with lemon extract.

And, speaking of AIDS hoaxes, just last week a phony report was published in the Melrose (Wisconsin) Chronicle about a central Wisconsin dairy farmer under investigtion for transmitting AIDS to his cattle.

It was bogus, of course. A gullible newspaper editor took the bait of a phony *USA Today* story.

Funny?

No.

"I would not make jokes about AIDS," said Bricker.

AIDS victims can, he said, in the same way "black people can make jokes about black people. It can be a release of tension, and not mean-spirited. If they laugh it is their right, it's their own situation.

"But I doubt if they laugh very much," he said.

As for the AIDS message in a coffin, true or not, Bricker said "I can't think of a more horrible joke to play on someone."

■ **May 27, 1990**

Tragedy Leaves No Room for Blame

That was then; those were incidents. This is now; this is a tragedy.

In the little neighborhood—and it is a neighborhood—that is dissected by Badger Road and bordered by Fish Hatchery Road and Park Street, children skip, walk, trudge and sometimes wander to Lincoln School every morning. Shoelaces untied, carrying colorful backpacks, they cross Badger Road where Cypress Way ends. Other kids wait impatiently at a bus stop near Fiedler Lane and Badger Road.

Because Badger Road is such a busy road, a lot of Madison sees those kids right there, right then, every day.

Some of those children come out of a set of two-story buildings on Sommerset Circle, but known simply as Sommerset.

Generally, the public gets to know about a neighborhood because of the neighborhood festivals, block parties, clean-up campaigns and the like.

Sommerset has versions of those, surely and certainly, but the Madison public remembers Sommerset not for the social programs or neighborhood get-togethers, but for the incidents.

The public remembers the shotgun shooting, the sexual assault report, the cocaine spill, the fight, the cars vandalized, the embarrassing spectacle of the media covering the arrival of a free-food truck.

But there have been other notices about Sommerset, longer

ones, more detailed, positive ones. Ones where people vow to "change" Sommerset. Less than a week ago consultants said the turnaround is in the works, tenants were tired of bad actors and bad press.

No one outside of Sommerset remembers those stories. The first words in a discussion about Sommerset are too often focused on blame instead of what can be done. It's the residents' fault. It's the owner's fault. It's the police. It's the lack of police. It's the media. The buildings are built wrong. It's the non-residents.

In all those debates, in all those meetings, in all the talk, few remember that every morning children emerge from Sommerset to go to school, just like children everywhere else in this city.

Now remember the children only because five of them died in a fire.

And still there is the search for blame, even stronger now is the search for blame in the deaths of innocents.

There will always be children at Sommerset. There are few three- and four-bedroom apartments affordable to the potential residents of Sommerset.

Sommerset will not go away. It should stay. It should stay until the only news from Sommerset is an announcement of a neighborhood block party. It should stay because there are five fewer children there today and you can't just drive by Badger Road and Cypress Way in the morning without thinking about it.

All those other things, that was then, those were incidents, there is blame.

This, this is now, this is a tragedy.   ■ **March 14, 1990**

What? Nary a Protester in Sight?

*T*he answer is: Just a couple of old men fighting for money, that's why.

The question is: Why isn't someone in the city of protests protesting the boxing match in Madison Wednesday night?

The entertainment features Aaron Pryor, 34, a former boxing champion, against Daryl Jones. Pryor risks his eyesight by boxing.

I call it entertainment because professional boxing is not a sport. It's a crooked business, there's proof enough of that to go around, and it's not worth arguing about.

But in Madison?

Why no protests?

Why no letters to the editor? Why no occupation of the Department of Regulation and Licensing offices by irate students?

Why and who would protest?

■ If it were two spider monkeys fighting each other at the Masonic Temple Wednesday night, the animal rights zealots would be cranking up their fax machines and making midnight spray-painting raids on defenseless buildings. After all, this fight has nothing to do with possibly fatal experiments on living, breathing creatures, does it?

■ If the fight were held up because one of the promoters-fighters-managers-marketers was gay, there would be protests. But the sexual preferences of the fighters has not been made public (though everything else has), so two old men beating on each other is nothing for that group to protest about. And boxing has nothing to do with discrimination, does it?

■ If the fight were scheduled to take place on a Madison bicycle path, there would be a terrific protest from that group. Bicycling enthusiasts would show up wearing masks, of course, since they would not want to be identified for fear of being forced to pay $3 for bicycle licenses. After all, this fight has nothing to do with training and good health, does it?

■ The fight is not about pro-anti-abortion-choice-life, so the supporters on each side of that issue will not show up. After all, no one could get killed here, could he? No one is making uninformed medical decisions here, is he?

■ If the fight were being held in the Gates of Heaven synagogue or the Bethel Lutheran Church sanctuary, perhaps the high and mighty of Madison's religious leaders would lead a protest of blood being spilled in a sacred place. But this is only a Masonic temple, rented for shows and dances, not a church or a fishing pier, so there are no clerics on the sidewalk protesting this one. It's not like it was two adults having sex for money, something the moral police could sputter about.

■ If a union were being shut out of this fight, perhaps the locals would be protesting. But there is no contract wrangle here, is there? Nothing that would force a working person to do his or her job in conditions that could permanently injure?

■ If this were a fight between two low-level marijuana salesmen, the Justice Department would have a honed squad of fatigue-clad narcs infiltrating the event all the way to the cloak room. But no, nothing illegal about boxing, no gambling here.

■ If this were a fight between two mentally handicapped people, you can believe the health professionals would be waiting in the lobbies, urging legislation, maybe even a state-paid ombudsman, possibly even an investigation. But this isn't anything that might injure a participant's brain, is it?

No, no protests here in Madison. It's just a boxing match, some guys having a little fun for money. No harm. Anything for a buck, right? It doesn't hurt or affect animals, gay men, bicyclists, religion, abortion, women, mentally or physically disabled people, unions, medical professionals or sister cities.

Just a couple of old men beating each other to death or disability, for fun and profit in Madison, where protest is sometimes a self-service industry.   ■ **May 15, 1990**

Did She? It's Classified Information

*L*ooks can be deceiving.

I read the paper Sunday and saw the following classified ad under Lost-And-Found:

"LOST: 1/2 $100 BILL. Park St. Area. Reward. 873-4593."

It must be that Valentine's Day is coming, but I read romance and intrigue, even danger, in that ad.

Ah, I thought, strangers meet by chance on Park Street, they hit it off, exchange meaningful glances from across a crowded room, swear they will call one another the next evening and seal the deal by cutting a $100 bill in half, each keeping one half.

Or maybe the ad was a signal, agreed on long ago, for two lovers to meet again for a spaghetti dinner at Josie's on Valentine's Day in 1990, 25 years after they first met and were torn apart by forces over which they had no control, forces that mysteriously provided a $100 bill to prove identity, forces that mysteriously knew that a $100 bill would be worth about two Josie spaghetti specials in 1990.

Or maybe this was a drug deal, consummated with the ceremonial cutting of the $100 bill—probably called a "C-note" by a couple of mugs talking in the back seat of a car driven by "Rico"—and the reminder "you'll get the other half when you deliver."

But no.

This was even more complicated.

This involves a two-year-old named Marsha, and it involves her reputation, which has left her looking like the ultimate of power munchers.

Marsha is the daughter of Sheila Michaelis and Sernell Williams, of Stoughton. Michaelis, contacted Monday morning at work at the Famous Footwear Distribution Center, provided a description of what led to the missing one-half of a $100 bill.

A week ago Monday, Williams drove to Madison in his Pontiac station wagon, on his way to Meriter Hospital-Madison General with an ill infant and two other pre-schoolers.

In the front seat was Marsha.

Williams stopped first at Park Bank to get grocery money, in the form of one $100 bill, which he placed in the front seat between the seats, with the checkbook.

He got to the hospital, unloaded the kids and went in. Then he realized he left the money and checkbook in the car.

"He went to get it off the seat and all he could find was half of a hundred dollar bill," said Michaelis.

"We ripped the whole car apart looking for it. I mean, that was our grocery money. We went home and counted pennies."

They also went home and watched Marsha's diaper very carefully, thinking what a waste of money.

"We watched but it never showed up," said Michaelis.

Purely hearsay evidence, of course, but Marsha "has been known to eat paper," said Michaelis.

"It looked like a clean rip, to me, though," Michaelis said.

"And she does a real good job on books and magazines."

They searched the car again, and again.

It wasn't thrown out the window, because the car windows were closed.

But it might be out there, and a finder could remove the blot on Marsha's reputation, so Michaelis took out the ad.

"I figure, if you saw half-a-hundred dollar bill you would probably pick it up and hang on to it for a souvenir. I'll give them $20 if they give it back to me.

"What did we do with our half? We wrote our name and the date on it and stuck the half-a-hundred away.

"When Marsha gets old enough she can see it and get a good laugh out of it. Either that or we could have her pay it back," Michaelis said, laughing.

As for Marsha, for now she's stuck with the reputation of a girl with expensive tastes.

◼ **February 13, 1990**

The Virtues of Growing Up in the Lutefisk Belt

*O*K, first the lutefisk joke.

"In the Viking times, you knew you were going to have a bad day if you woke up in your little village and smelled lutefisk, because that meant the Viking ships were only about 10 miles away."

The teller is Bill Andresen, president of Olfisk Inc., of Minneapolis.

I called him because of an unidentified advertisement that showed up in the newspaper last week. The large ad said simply: "Holidays, Family and Lutefisk, Keep the Tradition."

The rest of the ad included four suggestions on how to prepare and eat lutefisk. One of the suggestions was how to disguise lutefisk so even children will eat it.

Another suggestion was to put the lutefisk along with mashed potatoes on a piece of lefse, which is also made of potatoes. Only a Norwegian would garnish his potatoes with potatoes. ("And for dessert, potatoes and ice cream!") The ad did not say where to buy lutefisk, who to buy it from or how much it costs. Nor did it contain a "cents-off" coupon for lutefisk.

The ad was placed by Andresen.

It was part of a deal he made with the Norwegian Stockfish

Exporters Association, which agreed to the simple, generic ad so that competitors would not get mad at each other.

"We placed the ad in all the papers in the lutefisk belt, Madison, Mason City, Fargo, Bismarck, Duluth," Andresen said.

Madison has been called a lot of things, but this was the first time I had ever heard it in association with the "lutefisk belt."

Andresen's company sells about 250 tons of lutefisk annually all over the country. He just shipped three tons to New York City (the Italians love it, he said.) To Madison this year he will send more than 15 tons.

Andresen is one of the three remaining "soakers" in Minnesota. A "soaker" soaks the imported Norwegian dried cod for two to three weeks to make it, according to some tastes, edible.

Lutefisk is dried fish treated with lye, an age-old "preservation and reconstitution" process that allows the dried fish to "reabsorb" the water.

Jokes, whole books even, have been written at the expense of lutefisk, which has gone full circle in the food business: from a staple, everyday meal to a traditional holiday meal.

Andresen sells "Viking" brand lutefisk to churches in the Madison area. Once a year he shows up in Madison to join Jim Soderholm of Soderholm Wholesale Foods, on a tour of area churches, looking for lutefisk business.

No one runs through town announcing that "The lutefisk salesman is here, the lutefisk salesman is here," but Soderholm said they are met with friendliness and good cheer all around.

Lutefisk sells for about $2.89 a pound, said Soderholm, who ran out of the product Thursday and had to arrange an emergency truckload.

Soderholm took over the lutefisk customers of the late Henry

Ullsvik, an East Washington Avenue grocer and for many years the Lutefisk King of Madison.

How's it selling?

Well, two weeks ago at the Lakeview Lutheran Church's lutefisk dinner, they came back for more twice and sold 1,600 pounds worth. In Barneveld Saturday, the Barneveld Lutheran Church ordered 1,225 pounds for its annual dinner.

Notice how this column has said (mostly) nice things about lutefisk?

Notice how I have not said what the stuff looks like when it is ready to be eaten? (This is a morning newspaper. People are eating breakfast while reading this.) Notice how I have not recounted the number of torturous trips to Lutheran churches in Westby and West Salem I was forced to take on cold winter nights as a child. For all of these trips, I acquired only a love for lefse, meatballs, pastries, creamed peas, boiled potatoes and lingonberry sauce with cream.

Notice how I have not told my favorite (true) story about dried fish, the story about the tons of dried fish shipped from Norway to an African country, which did not realize it was fish until after it rained. The dried fish had been used for roof shingles.

No, you won't hear any badmouthing of lutefisk from this corner.

If there is one thing lutefisk does for you, it teaches you restraint. ■ **November 17, 1987**

Main King Tap "Family" Has Last Day

A mother cradles her two-year-old daughter in one corner, kissing her, finding her bottle, telling her it is 9 o'clock, time to go.

In another corner, so dark that the atmosphere sticks to your pants cuffs, another deal is made, not so quietly, and the juke box blares on: "We are family . . ."

Good night forever, sweet Main King Tap, home of watery Old Milwaukee taps and tight-lipped bartenders, ash-blonde whores and pimps in orange pants, pin-striped Johns and spaced-out Janes.

Oh, mister bartender, give me a 7-and-7.

Tuesday night, last night, after a certain hour, you could leave your quarters soak on the sticky bar at the Main King Tap, 106 King Street.

Terry Rice, the bartender and owner, was slipping his regulars free drinks, swishing a bar rag, ringing up 40-cent tabs.

"This the last night, Terry?"

"Yeah, I'm going to slip out of town," he said.

Any last words?

"No way, I got enough ink the way it is."

"We are family . . ."

From the sign over the bar that says: "Attention Wino's. Wine $2.50 a fifth."

To John the drunk: "I'm the family drunk. Central High, 1950.

Second base. I've been 22 years in the Marine Corps and 12 years where you ain't got time to spend. I'm scared enough to be tough, man. They know me."

John sucks on a Pall Mall straight and squeezes the frost off of a glass of vodka and ice.

"Where'm I gonna go after this?" he asks.

"See that man," asks John, pointing to the man in blue windbreaker who is buying Old Style in cans, pouring the beer into a glass of ice. Smoking menthol.

"He's got money for women."

Indeed.

Surrounded by them, he is. Two white and two black. They stay. He leaves. They talk. One leaves.

Reflected in the smudged mirror behind the bar, Terry and Leonard draw taps, mix the simplest of drinks for the unseen clientele upstairs, forward hushed telephone calls, call taxis, cash suspicious "if-this-don't-go-I'll-see-you" checks.

Mr. Gray Pin Stripes walks in, a Miller Lite.

Mr. Flash follows, sticks a finger into the back of a leather-coated brother.

"Oh, my man."

In the shadow of the Capitol, man, when there's light to cast a shadow, but in the night there is no shadow, in the night there is only family.

"We are family . . ."

Terry the bartender knows it is his last night.

He wraps a bottle of vodka into a brown paper sack, twisting the sack around the neck of the bottle.

"This'll keep you 'til Christmas," Terry says to John, the family drunk.

"I've been drinking here for 30 years," says John.

"Off and on," reminds Terry.

"Corn curls and orange juice," is the soft order from a redhead with hollow eyes, nice raincoat, lots of finger rings. It's the last bag of corn curls on the wall.

Two cops walk in. Terry asks that they be in the area at midnight.

"We're done at midnight. They told me to close for good at midnight. The party don't start 'til we close," he says.

The Main King Tap is in the process of being sold, and the new establishment is being planned as a "Victorian-Irish pub and restaurant."

The Main King Tap closed at midnight Tuesday, April 1, 1981.

■ **April 1, 1981**

Never Forget What It Is Like to be Unemployed

*O*ne of the things you do when you are out of work is check your wallet often.

Even when you know it is empty, you check it. For the 10th time: Maybe there is a five-spot in the secret compartment you forgot about.

When there is money in your wallet, you know exactly how much there is. People who are out of work or luck tend to know, sometimes to the quarter, how much money they are carrying.

It is time we remembered when we were looking for jobs and there were none to be had.

Some don't have to remember any further back than today.

You don't have to send the TV crews to Janesville, or Beloit, to find the unemployed. They are everywhere.

Nearly every family can tell you about a brother, a son, a daughter, a nephew, an uncle, an aunt, who is looking for work.

Here is a reminder of what it is like, without the statistics, without the graphs or the pronouncements of experts.

When you are out of work you keep lists of where you spent what, and you get mad if your wife doesn't remember or didn't keep the sales slip.

When you're out of work, sometimes, you turn down dinner invitations and say that you're busy. You think they invited you because you're out of work.

You get darn tired of people asking you if you've "found anything yet."

You get darn tired of weepy television shows and news photos of people standing around in the streets warming their hands over a smoking trash barrel.

You're not in the street. You're not a bum at a trash can. It's not the same.

You're darn tired of having to prove you're poor and unemployed. Of having to sign something to prove you are eligible, for anything. You don't enjoy this, you don't want to be here, doing this, proving you deserve something.

You don't want to hear, ever again, someone who can't know how you feel say "I know how you feel."

You're tired of macaroni and cheese, tuna fish casserole, meatloaf, tomato soup and white socks you buy six to a package.

You make a lot of unfair judgments. You hate restaurant reviews, and you hate game shows and success stories and any-thing labeled "motivational."

You hate putting things off because you can't afford them.

You begin disliking anything new, pretty, big, colorful, expen-sive or even clean.

You don't like people who have two jobs when there aren't enough to go around for you to have even one job.

You hate your empty postbox, your empty 'fridge, your empty gas tank.

You hate having a lousy, cynical, defeatist attitude and you are only vaguely aware of what is going on, how this is eating you up.

And most of all, deep inside, you hate having to take this sympathy, these promises of prosperity and a better "future."

If you get a job, you will remember all that, not because you want to, but because it is something you can never forget.

■ January 30, 1983

Ferry Tragedy Really Hits Much Closer to Home

It is near impossible to travel anywhere in Scandinavia without traveling at least once by ferry.

For many travelers, the ferry itself—offering gambling, inex-pensive drinks, tax-free purchases and entertainment—is the destination.

For others, especially permanent residents of those high-tax northern countries, the ferry is a necessity, providing passage at reasonable cost to another country where simple foodstuff and other items are cheaper.

So it is that the fire and deaths on a Scandinavian car ferry is an insidious tragedy. Last Friday two fires started or were deliberately set on the Scandinavian Star, which has be traveling on a regular route between Oslo, Norway, and Frederikshavn, Denmark, for less than a month. (It was last in duty out of Miami.) So far, the fatality list is 150 and counting. Counting, because police are just now finding the children who are not usually included on a passenger list. So the estimate was 170 dead Monday, maybe 200 by Tuesday. Maybe more.

This tragedy is closer to us, to Americans, even to Wisconsin residents, than many may think.

A woman in this office, for example, was with her husband on that very ferry route three weeks ago.

The many college students and vacationers who travel to Europe in the summer can hardly avoid a ferry if they have northern Europe in their sights.

And with the high-percentage of Scandinavian immigrant descendents in Wisconsin, it is not difficult to imagine that relatives of this state's residents were on that ferry last Friday.

On my first trip to Norway, in 1971, I arrived on a ferry from Newcastle to Bergen. When I left Norway for good in 1976, newly married, I left on a ferry from Oslo to Copenhagen.

That ferry, in fact, was often used by university students for weekend trips because of the high cost of living in Oslo. It was cheaper for a student, using a 50-percent rebate, to take the ferry that left at about 5 p.m. on Friday from Oslo, arrive in

Copenhagen at about 7:30 a.m. Saturday, goof off in Copenhagen all day, take the 5 p.m. Saturday ferry from Copenhagen, arrive back in Oslo Sunday morning. Food and drink were tax-free on the ferry and a couple of bottles of tax-free wine were brought back for special occasions.

Now, my wife and sons take the Horten to Moss ferry, Basto, across the Oslo fjord a couple of times each summer to visit her sister on the Swedish border. We drive in to the basement of the boat, where cars and trucks are packed bumper to bumper and door to door, then spend the half-hour or so upstairs drinking coffee and watching the coast.

Today, the governments of Norway, Sweden and Denmark are investigating the cause of the deaths of perhaps 200 people. They need to look at whether people were illegally sleeping in their cars instead of heading to the upper decks overnight. They need to look at charges the crew could not speak any Scandinavian language so could not communicate with passengers, and that the crew was not trained to handle a fire, and that the ferry ship was sailing under a Bahama registry, which allowed less stringent safety regulations.

This is another one of those tragedies that is in the headlines for only a brief time because there was, as the television reports say, "only one American victim."

Maybe not.   ■ **April 11, 1990**

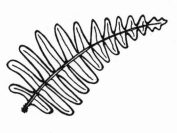

Going Door to Door—
You Can Knock It
If You've Tried It

I hate going door to door.

I hated it when I sold Christmas cards door to door as a boy. I hated it when I had to sell band candy, Cub Scout first-aid kits, garden seeds and spray-on ointment. I even hated collecting the dimes for delivering the Sunday St. Paul *Pioneer Press.*

I hated walking up to the front doors of people I knew just slightly or not at all. (Now there's a phobia for a future journalist.)

Funny though, there was never a question of not doing it, never even a question of skipping over a house.

(Tiny Mrs. Holts, for example, of an age over 90, lived alone in a large corner house. She never bought anything but she would have been offended if not asked.)

Then there were the people who answered the door and you were the last person in the world they wanted to see. On some nights, it went from dour to dour.

Three recent happenings brought back these memories.

My sons' child-care provider has fund-raising events. Candy for sale, puppets for sale, hopscotch contests. I think ages three and six are too young to be used as a front, even if those puppets are cute.

Then, while I was raking some of the smallest boulders from

the front lawn one evening last week, a neighbor walked by with her teen-age son. I hadn't seen her in a while so we chatted about this and that while the boy just stood there and looked uncomfortable.

At a pause, she nodded at the boy and said something like, "Well, we better get this part over with." And the boy, looking as if he had just been accused of wearing argyle socks, hauled out a brochure presenting candies for sale.

I bought some candy, the cheapest on the list ($5.50), though I don't like most candies and this was, after all, the week after Easter.

I told the kid I used to have to do that, and I hated it.

He nodded, kept his hands in his pockets. That's high school. What could he say?

Finally, last week I had to visit every house in the neighborhood to deliver design ideas for a neighborhood sign.

All the old fears, the old unanswered questions, came back:

■ The pained expressions when people first answer the door, thinking I was selling something or collecting for the latest cause. ("Here's your sign stuff," was all I could say.)

■ The point where I knew a person's name but couldn't remember it at the moment I needed to say it. ("Here's your sign designs, mmmmfph mmmfph.")

■ The houses that appear to have no entrances. Just how do people get into this house? Where do I knock? Can I walk on this grass? If there is no sidewalk to the door does that mean I can't walk here? If no one answers, do I put the material in the front door, which is probably only used by foreign wedding guests?

■ Being unable to hear the doorbell. If I can't hear it when I push the button, is it broken? Do I knock? How loudly? Is it rude to knock at a door equipped with a doorbell? Should I tell them the doorbell is broken? If all the lights are on, but no one answers the door, what are they doing in there?

I delivered to all but three homes because it got dark and the only thing worse than going door to door is going door to door in the dark.

Which brings up the question of Halloween and the joys of anonymous trick-or-treating at houses occupied by people who didn't buy Cub Scout ointment. ■ **April 26, 1990**

Hey, Adults, We're Not So Smart, Either

Just once I would like to see a story about a bunch of teen-agers who go out and survey adults on their knowledge of mathematics, geography and spelling.

Another report showed up the other day about how the written vocabulary of children in grades one through eight was two and a half times larger 40 years ago than it is today.

An analysis of 4,000 compositions found just more than 10,000 different words. A similar study conducted in 1945 yielded about 25,000 different words.

This Indiana University report also found that today's children are writing more about violence and drugs, and they are using a lot of different words than did the children of 1945. (No kidding.)

This report comes on the heels of others that tell us our children don't know where anything is and, if they did, they couldn't write a letter home about it.

So, aside from the usual hand-wringing and blaming it all on the teachers—parents get credit, teachers get blame, kids get it both ways, that's life—how about a little perspective?

Let's toss a few questions at the parents who cluck cluck about kids these days:

One. Neptune has how many moons?

Two. How many in a megabyte?

Three. What is the minimum wage for corn detasselers in Wisconsin?

Four. Name the Baltic States.

Five. What is Saigon now called?

Just ask those five questions for a start. Ask them of an adult over 30, even better if over 40. I'll bet four out of five adults get four wrong out of five.

Unfair? Certainly not. Adults should crack the books once in a while, too. Bones may stop growing, but brains shouldn't. We should be thankful students are too polite to ask these questions of their elders.

I am suspicious of leaders who use such survey tests as evidence that the problems of educating this generation can be solved if we can only get the kids to memorize landmarks of Western civilization. It is as if we are saying that we measure the success of education by whether a student acquires enough plastic pastel wedgies in a game of trivia.

Not that landmarks of Western civilization are all trivia.

Perhaps we could mix the questions up a bit. Add a few relevant questions, such as:

One. List five synonyms for "dude."

Two. What is the most difficult letter of the alphabet to shave into the side of your head?

Three. What are shoelaces?

Four. A flipper is to pinball what a -------- is to Nintendo.

There's a thought.

Before any test results of students are released to the media, the same tests should be given to members of school boards in those students' districts, and the results can be reported simultaneously.

Then perhaps the students can stand around coffee shops and bars and cluck cluck about the sorry decline of standards in adult education these days.

■ ■ ■

ANSWERS, Part I : One. At least six moons for Neptune. Two. A million in a megabyte, or, more accurately, 1,048,576 bytes. Three. The state minimum wage for agriculture workers, minors, is $3.25 an hour. The federal minimum wage for detasselers is $3.80 per hour. (Use of the higher wage depends on the size of the operation.) Four. Estonia, Latvia, Lithuania. Five. Ho Chi Minh City.

ANSWERS, Part II : One. There are no synonyms for dude. Two. B. Three. Not Applicable. Four. Joystick.

■ **April 17, 1990**

Family

A Suitcase
Santa Would Envy

The suitcase was packed and I was doing the inspection.
First, I noticed a little white plastic bag that clanked.
I did not remember packing any handcuffs or socket wrench
sets in my wife's suitcase for her trip to see her parents in
Norway, so I opened the bag with her permission.

It contained six cans of Nine Lives cat food, the type we feed
our cats only on holidays. Stuff like sirloin tips in Bernaise sauce
with cod flavoring.

My wife's sister, Rikke, a schoolteacher in a small town on
the Norwegian side of the Norway-Sweden border, has a cat,
it turns out. In old-fashioned Norway, the cats are expected to
earn their keep and there are few cat foods to choose from,
certainly none as exotic as what Nine Lives serves up.

So Else, my wife, was taking some of the more interestingly
titled—and expensive—tin goods to Rikke's kitty.

The next package I inspected contained four big bags of chocolate chips.

This was a questionable import, since, considering the
scrumptious sjokolade available there, taking chocolate chips to
Norway was like taking beer to Monroe.

Well, explained Else, when her sister and parents visited here
three years ago, they liked the chocolate-chip cookies we baked,
but to bake chocolate chip cookies in Norway they would have
to sit and hack off little chips from a block of chocolate. The
result: non-uniform chips in a chocolate-chip cookie.

So, into Else's suitcase went four pounds of Nestle's best

morsels.

In the next bag, I found two pounds of Wisconsin sharp cheddar cheese.

This I could understand.

Next bag: A liter of Johnnie Walker Black Label for my father-in-law, Oddvar, who is one of the last of the craftsmen stonecutters in Norway. This was easy to understand, too, since the bottle that cost $20 here cost three or four times that much in the state-controlled liquor stores of Norway. Also, a bottle of sherry and two cartons of Pall Mall straights.

The rest of the stuff was packed in Sunday newspaper comic pages, but Else said the packages contained the usual gifts of clothes and stuff, including a Milwaukee Brewers sun visor for my sister-in-law's husband, Oystein, who wouldn't know a Milwaukee Brewer from a Milwaukee streetlight but who likes to wear those things to confound the villagers.

Since Oystein is forever haunting book shops looking for old books, I also sent him the title page and first five chapters of a book I picked up at an auction: the second edition in Norwegian of Charles Dickens' Oliver Twist, 1862. (This is a mutual exchange, since he keeps a lookout for old umbrellas for my collection.) Else also took along 20 packs of Doublemint gum for herself because she quit smoking two months ago.

She didn't mind filling her only suitcase with this stuff because she will be bringing it back filled with things you can't get here.

At the top of her list is Stabbur Leverpostei, which is sort of canned braunschweiger. She also is bringing back a bunch of rekeost, which is a shrimp spread for bread that comes in a toothpaste tube.

Still, since it is a tradition for our suitcases to be sent to the wrong places, I have visions of Else's plaid suitcase showing up in a hot unclaimed baggage room in Bangkok, Thailand, where I once stayed for three weeks without seeing a single cat, much less a hungry one. ■ **July 31, 1983**

New 'Dude' Gives Hope to the World

*E*lse tip-toed out of the baby's room.

"The dude has zonked," she announced with a whisper that carried the same prideful emphasis as if she had said "The Eagle has landed."

What she meant, of course, is that the baby is asleep.

But we are the new generation of babymakers and we don't say things like "the baby is asleep."

We are in our 30s—early 30s—and we have lived through the 1970s, when we and all of our friends were saying things like, "I would never bring a child into a world like this."

Well I haven't seen much change for the better in the world since then, but here we are and here is our dude, who in five months has convinced us that the world has a chance.

So far, he has found scant intellectual nourishment from our vocabulary. It is, I fear, another bit of flotsam from the non-communicative 1970s.

His name is Espen, a fine old Norwegian name, and most of the time I call him that.

But other times I call him other, normal names. I picked up the habit when I got my first kitten 13 years ago. The name was Gulliver, but I changed it as often as the campus mood shifted or if a girlfriend didn't like it. He was Gulliver most of the time, but he had other names too, like Harvey or Fred.

So Espen once in a while is Harvey, or Fred, even Oscar.

And then there is "dude."

When I get home from work and Else is there, my first question is "what's shakin' with the dude?"

Poor Else. Brought up in Norway and spirited away at the tender age of 26 to this land of immigrants, her English was perfect when she got here.

Now she answers me: "He's zonked, what a dude, eh?"

Say that with a Norwegian accent.

I have to learn different kinds of affection, too.

My standard line for people I like is, "Fire up, kid."

So I say to Espen, when he's not zonked, "Fire up, kid."

It's not as bad as something like, "I dig you the mostest," but it's not exactly "kootchy-koo," either.

We have little chats, though at five months Espen sometimes misses a few nuances of my logic.

"So what's happenen' Harvey?" I will ask, throwing in a joke like, "Did you change the oil in the car today?"

"Gerble-gooble, weeeow," says Espen, dribbling spit in a wire-fine line of Guinness length.

"No lie, I hear ya," says I.

We have probably been the closest so far, Espen and I, the Saturday I accompanied my music-crazy neighbor Tom to State Street so he could sell a couple of albums.

There, in the rack of a used record store, for $3.95, was an album called "Nelson Eddy and Jeanette MacDonald sing love songs."

My kind of entertainment, and as I recall, the first of my possessions I ever wanted to share with my son.

I came home, carefully slid the record on to the turntable, put on my headphones and sang love songs, accompanied by Nelson and Jeanette, to my son for 30 minutes.

I wailed. Espen wailed. Else took a hike.

Just as well, me and the dude were bonding. Sometimes a father and son have to do that. ■ July 10, 1984

House Now Safe, Sort of . . .

*D*ear Holiday House Guest: As you may have noticed, things have changed around here.

First, what you tripped over when you walked in the front door was a booby trap designed by either Fisher Price or Playskool. It has been found to be safe for children, but will crack the kneecap of anybody who can walk, and, it follows, trip and fall.

Next, you may have noticed the white pine one-by-two fence attached with clothesline cord to the iron railing that separates the living room from the stairway to the entrance where you just tripped and fell.

The fence looks a little low, but was designed and built by

me to keep things like Playskool and Fisher Price booby traps from being dropped onto the stairway.

You might have remarked privately about the lack of knobs and dials on the stereo receiver. This was another safety measure, to protect adult ears from what has become an unexpected decibel increase that occurs from time to time. It also protects bare skin from being scalded when those unexpected noise increases occur while drinking a cup of coffee at 6:30 a.m.

Oh yes, the toilet paper. We do keep toilet paper, but we keep it on the shelf right next to the toilet flush lever.

No, the kitchen cabinet doors are not stuck. Anyone capable of exerting 120 pounds of downward pressure on a tiny white plastic latch with one finger can open those doors.

Sorry there wasn't any ice for your drink. That cube you took from the tray in the freezer was frozen apple sauce.

We decided to put the Christmas tree in the garage. Looks great there, don't you think? It looks so natural, without ornaments.

Yes, the cats do look like they lost weight. That fur on the tail grows back, I'm told.

Oh, before I forget, here's that magazine article I've been saving for you. It's taped together in a few places and the third page is missing, but I think you can still get the gist of it.

Well now, it's getting late, isn't it. Must be nearly 8 o'clock. We turn in early these days.

By the way did I tell you it looks like our new son will be walking pretty soon? We can hardly wait.

■ **December 10, 1984**

Parents Purrfectly Surprised

We waited at the edge of our seats.

It was clear we were about to hear our son's First Word.

He reached up, extending both hands, grasping.

Our eyebrows went up. We twisted our faces into what we thought were looks of encouragement. What would the word be?

He had already mastered his own variations of "ball" and "shoe."

We were waiting for the important word, the one that would recognize either "Pa-Pa" or "Ma-Ma."

Alas, it was to be neither of the above.

My son, Espen: a child of college-educated parents; a child of unquestionable intelligence, wit and seven teeth; a boy who, at the tender age of 14 months, was dextrous enough to dunk my regulation-size basketball into a pan filled with crankcase oil; an infant able to maintain a scholarly fascination with the depth of my belly button.

Yes, this wonder child was ready to speak, ready to acknowledge our impact on his formative months.

His mouth opened, then closed, forming an "m." Aha, here comes "Ma-ma," we thought.

It was: "Meow."

That's just great. I spend hours reading aloud to the kid from books with washable pages and he rewards me with "Meow"?

Else devotes uncounted days encouraging oohs, giggles and

ahs from the fellow and he responds with a plaintive "Meow?" The utterance almost started an argument. Until he meowed, our biggest argument about his upbringing had been over buying lace or Velcro shoes. (Father, common sense and laces, 0. Mother, high-tech and Velcro, 1.) We decided we had done nothing wrong.

We blamed it on Charlie and Watson, our cats. Espen, observant child that he is, obviously took note that whenever Charlie or Watson want something, they meow, and they get it.

When they want to go out, they meow. When they want to come in, they meow. When they want to eat, they meow. Sometimes, we admit, when the cats start meowing, we meow back.

Fortunately, Espen's vocabulary has quadrupled since his first meow. He has pretty much abandoned that word—except when his is talking to the cats—in favor of Pa-pa, ball, shoe, tick-tock and a clever unspellable word he made up for cookie.

We don't know how this will affect his development or his chances of getting into the College of His Choice, but we're not too worried.

We consider ourselves lucky we don't keep pet chickens.

■ **June 15, 1985**

Passing the Test

ithout knowing it, we are always testing our children. When I roll a rubber ball under the coffee table to

22-month-old Espen, I am really checking to see if he will someday be able to backhand a line drive at third base.

When I take a walk around the block and let him push his
own stroller, I am really seeing if he has the balance that will
enable him to tiptoe down a sideline with a game-winning punt
return.

When I help him open the pots-and-pans cabinet, I am testing
his potential musical proficiency.

So when the season's first snow fell last weekend, I unwit-
tingly administered yet another test.

After pulling the snow shovel from the garage rafters, it
occurred to me that shoveling snow is the ideal father-son chore.
Out there, against the elements, two guys and their snow
shovels, working together for the common good of the family
and the family car.

So I made him a snow shovel.

I took an old handle I had saved from a beat-up snow shovel
and sawed it off at about 18 inches. Then I took the plastic cover
from a five-gallon can of driveway sealer and cut out a square
piece. This was nailed to the handle, creating a miniature snow
shovel.

Out the door and into the snow came Espen. He was so bulky
looking that if his clothes hadn't been so colorful, I would have
stacked him with the firewood on the side of the garage.

He looked up at me, cheeks starting to color, eyes sparkling,
and I knew it was time for the test.

I handed him his new snow shovel.

Then, to show him how it worked, I took my shovel and
pushed some snow off the driveway. Now, he could show me
what he was made of. He could join me in the chore and we
would work, shoulder to shoulder, trading sidelong glances as

we silently judged the quality of one another's work.

He took that snow shovel and trudged to the middle of the driveway.

He stopped, put the snow shovel down, wedging it solidly in the snow.

Then he put both hands on the shovel handle.

Then he leaned on it.

And he kept leaning on it, watching, occasionally shifting positions, while I shoveled the driveway.

Though I was a little disappointed, close relatives—mostly my mother and the wives of my brothers—tell me the kid was just doing what comes naturally. They tell me that there will be further manifestations of this family trait. They tell me that soon, he will be able to make his entire body disappear when it comes anywhere near a snow shovel.

They seem to think that he was testing me.

■ **November 23, 1985**

Sidekick
An OK Guy, Too

I don't hanker, I haven't sashayed or mosey-ed in a while and no one I know would ever describe me as lanky.

But as I begin my third year of fatherhood, I have begun to think of myself as the Last Cowboy.

Clearly, my son is not going to be the cowboy type, or know

anything about cowboys.

In the foggy recesses of my Baby Boomer Brain are fading memories of my own childhood as a cowboy. I had a set of chaps, vest and cowboy shirt I got for a birthday present. I had Roy Rogers pajamas, with a six-gun design. I had a black cowboy hat. I ducked behind imaginary boulders and snapped off a few rounds at the rustlers. I went to Fort Dells and saw the shootout.

I recently unveiled to my son my old Gene Autry puzzle. He liked the horse but could not identify with the cowboy.

The other Saturday morning we were watching Hopalong Cassidy, a bright spot on Saturdays thanks to WHA. He showed no interest whatever, this time even in the horses.

I tried to explain the right-wrong, white hat-black hat ethical symbolism of it all, using a glow-in-the-dark dinosaur as the bad guy and a Smurf as the good guy. (Hey, I'm flexible.) We had worked on good guys and bad guys before, but I think the Smurfs confused him. Why would a Smurf beat up a plastic dinosaur?

The point is, how will I teach him good from evil? These new children's shows seem to mix them all up. The characters transform. I know, there is good and evil in all of us, but starting out, shouldn't this be more clear cut?

With Hopalong, Gene Autry, Roy and Dale, the forces of evil were pretty obvious. Anyone who insulted the schoolmarm, was mean to his horse, stopped the stagecoach, threw his gun when it ran out of bullets, put anything on the train tracks or worked in a land office, was evil.

Anyone who was polite to ladies, had chrome on his saddle, wore two guns instead of one, shaved every day and was able to board a moving horse, was good.

Anyone who fell into the horse trough was a sidekick.

The big difference, now that I have spent a few minutes

thinking about it, was that the bad guys did not have names for their horses.

I worry a lot about good guys and bad guys.

It has not been all that easy telling the difference. I remember how confused I was when Paladin showed up on *Have Gun, Will Travel.* He wore all black working clothes, was kind to his horse and had a good guy sense of humor. He looked like a bad guy and acted like a good guy.

The safest route, I think, is to go the sidekick route. First, the sidekick sometimes got both the girl and the horse. He was always late to the big shootouts and thus was never seriously injured. He got to go in to town and hang out a lot. He sometimes knew a few basic magic tricks.

It is all very well to extoll the virtues of the white hats and throw peanuts and boo the black hats. But I was not far into my early cowboy education before I started making little judgments.

Nobody is that good, I thought, and I later discovered that to be true.

And some people aren't that bad, I thought, and later discovered that to be true.

I also discovered there are more bad people masquerading as good people than there are good people masquerading as bad people.

So I guess I'm not the last cowboy after all, and I won't represent myself as that to my son. I'll continue to call him pardner, though, and try to raise him to be a good, though non-aligned, sidekick who doesn't mind falling in the horse trough once in a while.

With luck he will be able to hanker and mosey with the best of them.   ■ March 22, 1986

Springtime Invites Father-Son Outing

O n a sunny springtime Friday I pick up the dude early from day care, strap him to the front seat and set off to introduce him to Festge County Park.

We have what we need: A box of McDonald cookies, two extra diapers and plastic pants, a baseball cap each, and trousers with pockets for rocks.

On a nice day, the road to Festge's is a short one. In days past, it was a great, short, motorcycle ride. Now it is a father-son ride in a rusty old Mazda.

Straight out to Middleton on University Avenue, the bumpiest of all avenues, past the new hidden condos on the left after Perkins. Espen at this age is interested in cows, horses, dogs, buses, tractors and flags, so Perkins is always a notable monument in our travels.

Fortunately, we have never seen a dog driving a tractor pulling a horse trailer with a flag on it, following a bus.

Driving through Middleton is more fun now that the roads are repaved.

We cruise out 14, past the remodeled Fish Building Supply. Things are greening everywhere. Lots of tractors in dusty fields.

We're going 55 and the guy behind us is going 56, aching to hit 65. There are times like this when I wish I still had the old Buick Electra, which was so beat up another dent or two wouldn't have mattered. It was a car built for the Park Street-Regent Street intersection, where dunderheads, usually driving cars with vanity plates, attempt to slip into the left (and correct) lane by steaming out of the right lane.

The Buick was undefeated in dunderhead racing at Park and Regent.

Our cruise continues through Cross Plains, past the grocery store with the ring of bologna on its sign, past the "Gopher Crossing" sign. I have never met a cross person in Cross Plains.

A couple of miles out of town is a hard right turn up a steep hill that leads to Festge County Park. One other car is parked here. We watch a middle-age couple wander up the path from the woods. Espen spots the horses on the swing set and he must ride them all, and the merry-go-round horses, and the slide.

The next hour or so is spent watching, from the lookout, the big trucks power along the highway. Then it's back to the car for a coast down the hill and over to the pond next to Black Earth Creek across the road.

We load up with rocks and spend another hour eating our cookies and making little splashes in the big pond.

For those two hours, we didn't care about anything else. We didn't have to.   ■ May 11, 1986

And Baby Makes Three

spen and I take a walk just about every night at 8. We walk to the end of the driveway and we stop.

Though there is seldom any traffic on our street, we always stop.

"Any cars on the right?" I ask.

"No cars," comes the answer.

"Any cars on the left?"

"No cars."

Then we say together: "Let's get outta here."

And off we go around the block, stopping in front of the same house every time to admire the flowers, stooping down so we don't hit our heads on the same branches of the same tree on the corner.

We will, at least three times along the route, both sit on our haunches and say together slowly: "Ready. Set. Go." Which is the start of a 10-yard race that I always lose.

We will be quiet or whisper in front of a couple of houses with dogs known to charge the street and scare the suspenders off of little boys and their dads.

We will stop in front of several driveways to admire the sealing job.

At least twice we will sing "One-two-buckle-my-shoe" up to 10. AT 10 we both break into hysterics singing "nine-ten-the BIG FAT HEN."

Figure at least two long stops to look at a squashed toad or chipmunk.

At the half-block marker, we will be near the horse pasture, so we have to comment on the horses, usually their eating habits.

At the three-quarter block marker, we will detour to a dead end to look at a flag in the neighbor's yard.

It is in the last quarter-block that anything can happen. Sometimes we will be airplanes buzzing home for a landing in the driveway. Or we will practice walking backwards. Often, that last stretch will be walked with Espen seated on my shoulders, getting a better view of things, trying to screw my cap on tighter.

There are other little chores that have been lightened by making a routine out of them.

For dinner, we wash our hands by the "me-first" method.

Else will say "dinner's ready."

And I'll suggest we go wash our hands, usually without getting an answer.

Then I'll say: "Me first."

The response is always: "No, me first."

This shouting match continues in a galloping dash to the bathroom, where Espen climbs up on the two-step stool and we put the plug in and turn on the water.

"Wait 'til it gets warm," I'll say.

"Wait 'til it gets warm," Espen will say.

We wash up and Espen always gets to pull the plug out.

Most of these conversations take place in half-Norwegian, half-English, just as the final conversation does in our hand-washing ritual.

"Ren og pen gutt," I'll say.

"Ren og pen," he'll say, and run into the dining room to show off his clean hands to Momma.

"Ren og pen gutt" means "clean and neat boy."

Anyway, we took the walk again the other night and as we buzzed into the driveway he noticed the sign I painted Thursday morning and planted in front of the half-barrel full of rain-soaked petunias and begonias.

"What's that?" he says.

"That's a sign, and it says 'It's a Boy,'" I say.

It says that and means a lot more.

It means that instead of two of us saying "me first," there

will be three.

It means pretty soon we will have someone else join us on these one-two-buckle-my-shoe walks.

It should be an easy route; we already know all the good spots.

■ **September 14, 1986**

Three Big Events on Thanksgiving

There are three important things going on this long weekend: eating a Thanksgiving meal, reading the advertisements and welcoming King Olav to Iowa.

In order, then.

We talk a lot about eating at my house these days, mostly with Espen in mind, and Thanksgiving will not be any different.

Espen, my son, is nearly four years old and he lives on air. He won't eat anything unless it is a nugget of some kind. On the night in question—that is, the night I said something I thought I would never say—he wouldn't even eat the chicken nugget.

He had already refused to eat cheese, yogurt, hash browns and beans. His favorite milk glass had gone untouched, except for the fork being swished along the bottom. When he took a bite, the food, to use an old Norwegian saying "grew in his mouth."

The usual bribes and threats were unheeded. Finally, I pulled the last straw.

"There are children starving in India," I said.

"Indiana?" he asked.

"No, India," I said.

He did not respond with something cute.

He did not wonder aloud—as I did when I was a boy—how we could wrap up and send this food to India without it getting cold or the package leaking.

He simply would not eat anything.

I worry more about his non-eating habits than I do about my trousers shrinking, my hair leaving, my knees getting stiff, my woodpile tipping over, my driveway cracking or my chicken pox scar showing.

We agonize over this nightly.

Exasperated, we have turned to the Flintstones for nutrition and the fake telephone call to Santa Claus for influence.

It would help if there was logic to these eating problems.

Why, for example, will he inhale a cheeseburger—except for the pickle— but not touch a meatball?

Why does he hate bacon?

In short, why can't beans be more like Gummi Bears?

So that will probably be our Thanksgiving dinner, if we can somehow make a drumstick look like a Gummi Bear.

As to reading the ads, today (Thanksgiving) is a Big Day for newspaper advertising. Careers have been made selling these. There are at least 11 "inserts," or advertising sections, in today's paper.

I read them looking for mistakes and great or illogical descriptions or completely unnecessary items. (I know, it's unfair to snipe and I'm a cheap date."

Someday I hope to find an advertising mistake that will allow me to buy a VCR for $6.

The descriptions?

How about "luxurious" jewelry, or "carefree polyester?" Then there is the headline that introduces "video gift ideas to warm their hearts," and the advertised video movie is *Dirty Harry*.

The "Radar Baseball" looks like a neat gift. It tells you how fast the ball was traveling when it was caught.

What is "Nordic" fleece? Is it warmer and does it come from a "Nordic" country?

What is a "dust indicator" on a vacuum cleaner? If you need one, should you be vacuuming in the first place?

Is it a selling point for dishes to be "refrigerator safe"? Can a plate be mugged by a refrigerator?

I would never buy anything described in words I can't understand, such as a "short-sleeve pad-dye knit pique shirt," or a jogging suit described as having a "basebally style collar with shoulder insert and two slash pockets."

What about these "four-hour only" sales?

What if I show up at 10:45 a.m., and before the sale ends at 11 a.m., I put something on sale in my cart, but don't get to the checkout until 11:30 a.m.?

I see by the ads that "Shaker" as in shaker-style sweater, is no longer capitalized? My dictionary says it should be.

Talk sexist to me: how about "men's boots" and "women's booties?"

There a sale on something called "retro" watches. For me that means they run backward, but the ad says simply they have "the timeless look of yesteryear."

As for King Olav of Norway, he is in Decorah, Iowa, this weekend. I met him at a party at his summer palace in 1971.

He probably doesn't remember me. I wore a leather coat and we talked about the weather.

So I owe him lunch. I thought about asking him over for Gummi Bears and turkey. We could read the ads, maybe go browsing for a Nordic fleece coat.   ■ **November 26, 1987**

The Urge to Smell Good

Around this time every year I get the urge to smell good. Buying cologne for Christmas is not as easy as it was in the days when we took our $1.50 down to Luedtke's Drugstore and bought a gallon of the latest smell, usually in a container that had a handle.

My son Espen and I were exposed to this change last weekend when we toured East Towne Mall looking for Christmas gifts.

Jennifer Riddle, a business reporter at the *State Journal,* had mentioned that she thought a cologne called Halston Z14, used by her husband, was "really hot."

This means very good.

Anyway, on the strength of Riddle's recommendation—and remembering that I had dumped 10 years worth of scented liquids down the toilet several years ago during a bathroom remodeling—I tipped off my wife Else, that I, too, wouldn't mind a "really hot" cologne.

After bluntly reminding me—as only a reformed smoker can do—that I would smell a lot better if I quit smoking cigarettes, she too sounded encouraging about the acquisition of a new smell for weekend and special-occasion use. I said I would check it out and, if it smelled OK, she might want to drop a couple of dollars for a pint of the new stuff.

So on a Sunday noon, Espen and I were standing in front of an untended fragrance counter of a large department store.

Halston Z14 was easy to spot on the shelves, but how could I find out what it smells like?

I asked a friendly clerk.

"Isn't there a tester out there?" she responded.

"What is a tester?" I asked.

She pointed to a box of bottles. All the bottles were of brands of cologne sold. A person interested in a particular brand could simply shoot a stream of that on to his wrist.

Unfortunately, the tester box didn't have any Halston Z14 in it.

The woman suggested that someone had stolen the tester.

Why would anyone do that?

"Oh, people do that all the time," she said, adding that the testers for the more popular fragrances were kept behind the glass counter because of thieves.

A woman at another fragrance counter in a different store said the same thing.

"Can you believe it? They're always ripping off the Polo tester," she said.

She didn't have a tester for the smell I wanted, either, but she opened a new bottle and gave me a whiff.

It was a sweet, limy smell that I wouldn't be caught vertical in.

We smelled a lot of testers Sunday and I didn't like any of them.

When my wife asked me what I really wanted to smell like, the best smell I could think of, the sexiest smell I can think of, is the smell of clean cotton sheets, fresh from the laundry line.

It may be one of the few smells they haven't been able to put into a bottle yet. ■ **December 15, 1987**

Hunting Strange Ducks in Oregon Village

My four-year-old son, Espen, and I went hunting recently for ducks in the village of Oregon.

We knew which ducks we were looking for: Donald, Daisy, Uncle Scrooge and the nephews.

After visits to five stores, we were able to find only some Smurf comics and the usual, run-of-the-universe Revenge of the He-Men Warriors stuff.

Then we wandered into the Oregon Pharmacy and a nice lady led us down an aisle, around a corner, and there was a whole rack of Donalds. We bought two and promised to be regular customers.

This happened before I found out I could have bought 14,000 comic books from the Internal Revenue Service, cheap.

The IRS is not known as a clearinghouse for comic books, but it seems a Toledo collector missed a few payments and the IRS confiscated his comic book collection. The government then bought an ad in the Comic Buyer's Guide, published in Iola, Wis., and widely read in Madison, a comic-heaven.

The IRS was offering to sell "13-14 thousand Silver Age to present comics. Marvels, DCs, some alternate titles. A wide assortment of Comics somewhat heavier in Marvels for the early years." The ad gave a number to call, ordering the buyer to ask for Steven Robinson, revenue officer in Ohio.

This was not easy. Robinson would talk about the comics only if "public affairs" allowed him to, which it did after considering for four hours the potential danger public disclosure of a comic book sale might do to the economic fabric of the country.

Robinson said he was the officer handling the tax collection case, so he was the person in charge of selling the 14,000 comic books. Actually, he described the case as "my taxpayer," and the comics as "my asset."

He said he was not allowed to talk about the case itself, but could talk about the comics.

He sounded eager to dispense his newly acquired knowledge, admitting he knew little about comic books before this sale.

Now, when someone asks if he's "got any turtles," he knows the questioner is talking about Teen-age Mutant Ninja Turtles, a comic book of extra value.

"I had to do some research, talk to dealers, and to the people who wanted to buy the comics," he said.

Mostly, they called, asking specific questions about specific comics that might be in the collection. He would get telephone messages that read: "Got a Spiderman 8?"

He found that people in the comic-collecting business could tell if he had a good collection simply by asking for two or three specific comics. If they weren't in the collection, the chances were that other valuable issues would not be, either.

He could have decided to sell the books one at a time. Instead, he decided to sell the whole bunch at once.

"It was a bulk situation, but more quantity than quality," he said.

"A few of the books might have been worth $40 or $50, but not many," he said.

"It would have made a fairly good opening stock for someone wanting to open a shop," he said.

He said the comics were "pretty standard stuff," from the early 1960s to the present. All were well-cared for, many kept in plastic covers.

Though he got telephone calls from 20 states, and several visits to the Federal Building in Toledo by prospective buyers, only six bids were received.

The 14,000 comic books sold for $3,000, or less than 25 cents each.

The two Donald comics Espen and I bought cost $1.25 each.

"I'm not surprised. No one is interested in buying that many comics unless the price is wholesale or less," said Robinson.

The $3,000 doesn't sound like much anyway. Wouldn't the taxpayer in this case have gotten more for his goods if he had sold them himself?

"We attempt to get as much as we can for the government and to protect the taxpayer's position," said Robinson. "We encourage people to do that on their own, but when they procrastinate, and when there is an asset and it's not being used to pay taxes," then the IRS gets it, usually taking fewer than 60 days to sell it.

Robinson, 35, said he recognized a lot of the titles in the collection from his own comic-reading days.

"Most were super-hero type comics, from the early 1960s.

I was more of a Flash and Green Lantern reader myself."

As for Donald Duck, Robinson said he couldn't recall if there were any Donalds in the bunch. Espen and I will stick with the Oregon pharmacy, but we'll keep an eye out for specials at the IRS.   ■ **February 28, 1988**

Unifinished Business

I have a note here to write about how hilarious it is when my son Espen, age four, sings the Banana Boat song. He calls it the Banana Bread song, and thinks the words are: DAY OLD, DAYAYAYAY OLD."   ■ **April 28, 1988**

Thermostat Juggling Runs in the Family

It was a dark, stormy and cold morning.

From the comfort of my bed, I heard soft footsteps in the carpeted hallway.

The footsteps stopped, so I stumbled to the bedroom doorway and caught the flanneled felon, my wife, in the act.

"Hands off the thermostat," I growled.

And so it goes. This is the season for sneaks.

The kind who, like me, sneak into the hall and turn down the thermostat.

And the kind who, like my wife, sneak into the hall and turn up the thermostat.

The Great Thermostat Debate rages for yet another season. While the word "cheapskate" balances on my wife's tongue, the word "spendthrift" balances on mine.

"I can see my breath; I'm freezing," she says.

"Brush your teeth and put on a sweater," I mutter.

"Think of the children," she says.

"No fair bringing the children into this."

"But they're cold, too," she claims.

"Put sweaters on them," I say.

"It says 64," she notes.

"That thermostat is way off," I comment.

"Yes, it feels like 55," she contributes.

"I'm not cold," I say.

"You're never cold," she says.

"I can't afford to heat the Great Outdoors," I say, warming to the hyperbole.

But the argument has ended; the thermostat stays on 70.

The results are this: I keep sneaking around and turning the thermostat down. She keeps sneaking around and turning it up. We never tell each other when we are going to do this. We manufacture reasons to walk by the thermostat to see who has altered the reading last.

The thermostat juggling is used as a starting point for other household chores, even romance. If I am in need of an early morning snuggle, I might turn the thermostat down earlier in the evening and then remark how chilly it seems to be getting.

If Else wants to assure my mood, she will turn the thermostat down before I get a chance to turn it down. I know her mood improves as the temperature goes up.

On long winter days when everyone is home the woodstove will take over from the furnace. It will create a hot fire long enough for Else to grudgingly open the patio door to COOL THE PLACE DOWN.

This temperamental obsession doesn't stop in the house.

It continues in the car, where I tend to place the heat control and the fan somewhere in the low to middle range.

Else tends to place the heat control on B for Boiling and the fan on B for Blow Your Socks Off.

She wonders why I never wear the sweaters I get for Christmas (I'm never cold enough for them to be of any use) and I wonder why she keeps buying me sweaters (it's so cold in the house she wears them for survival).

■　　■　　■

On the art of selecting the proper snow shovel, it is with some embarrassment I admit to buying, for the first time, a plastic-bladed snow shovel last week at the local hardware store.

A few years ago, I couldn't go to a summer auction in Green, Dodge or Iowa county without a broken or bent snow shovel mysteriously ending up in my car trunk at the end of the day. Suddenly, this winter I was stuck with one old bent aluminum-bladed shovel and one 25-pounder with a 6-foot handle that only works downhill in up to 2 inches of new snow.

So I went on rounds to co-ops, department stores and

hardware stores looking for the perfect snow shovel. It had to be light, preferably not plastic, with a grip handle. And it had to sound right.

It is not easy to find a snow shovel that sounds right, especially if you are buying before it snows. No way to give it a tryout.

The sound has to be appealing when used in a rhythmic pattern of scrape-toss, scrape-toss, scrape-toss. With plastic there is a lower, not unpleasant, tone when used on blacktop. With a double-driveway, meaning at least three rows of left-to-right scrape-toss of snow up to five inches deep, a too-high pitched scrape tone in the early morning could wake the neighbors, wife and children.

But you can't hack away with a plastic shovel blade on half-melted ice, and there is no substitute for a steel shovel blade to get closest to the driveway surface.

And, to muddle this further, there is talk at the office of a new high-tech snow shovel with a high-tech crooked handle that is supposed to be a "back-saver, heart-saver."

Still, the balance and the fact that it felt good favored the plastic blade, and I bought for $13 a wooden-handled, orange-plastic-bladed shovel, similar to a grain shovel. A good scooper but probably not the greatest for pushing snow. The handle was attached to the blade with screws, not just hammered in. It's light, and I suspect that when a good snow falls, the shovel will respond with a low-pitched scrape, similar to the sound made when a car runs over a cardboard box and drags it a short distance down the highway.

I'll keep the aluminum shovel handy for use in the kids' room.

■ **December 18, 1988**

Go Fly a Kite - Back Then It Was Easier

We parked the car, grabbed our stuff and walked to the middle of the McGaw Park soccer field.

Within 15 minutes, my son Espen and I had destroyed two cheap plastic kites, purchased on impulse at Woodman's. Our kite string, purchased on purpose at the Oregon Ben Franklin store, had broken and been retied four times.

We also watched a patient man and woman and their children attempt to launch what looked like an ordinary kite, but which was controlled by two strings. The stunt kite did not get more than 10 feet off the ground and the two strings seemed to assure twice the chance of failure.

A father does not feel foolish galloping along pulling a kite that is actually in the air and shows signs of doing what kites are supposed to do.

But a father does feel foolish galloping along pulling a kite that is dragging and hopping along the ground.

The design of our two kites was the same. A plastic sheet attached to a three-piece plastic frame.

On one kite, the one with Snoopy on it, the sheet ripped from the frame almost immediately and was impossible to attach again.

On the other kite, the one with the dinosaur on it (how to make a million in the '80s: Put a dinosaur on anything and sell it) the frame bent and the brand-new string broke four times.

Espen took our failure quite well. In fact, he pronounced the kite a "piece of junk," and we dragged it over to the playground for a go at the swing set. For a five-year-old, he handled this much better than his 38-year-old father. I decided he was too young to hear about peanut butter kites.

When I was a boy, my older brother Jay and I each got a Jif peanut butter kite in the spring.

We would wait until the Jif peanut butter kites showed up in downtown Bangor at Kapanke's IGA, beg for Mom to buy some peanut butter so we could each get a free kite. The kite came rolled up in yellow paper around a pair of long sticks. Jay and I would take over the front porch, dig out last year's kite string and put together the kites. We would make a kite tail out of old strips of brown and yellow cotton torn from a sheet that was wrapped around our shoulders whenever we got a haircut.

Then we would walk across the railroad tracks in the back of the garden and on to the Bangor High School football field, where we would join other kids with their yellow triangle Jif kites and the odd kid with his box kite.

I called Procter and Gamble, which owns Jif, to ask about the kites, but no one knew anything about such a promotion 30 years ago. They sounded as interested in it as I suspect my son Espen would have been. No matter. They made a good kite that lasted more than 15 minutes.   ■ **April 27, 1989**

Sharing Work with Young Set - And Loving It

I was a little late getting home from work. I had stopped at a lumberyard to get a swing-set seat and some bolts that would fit through the four-by-four I had nailed to a couple of trees in the back yard.

It had been a trying week already, and the homemade swing set was starting to become a regular evening plague. Either the bolts were too short or the nails the wrong kind or the ladder not long enough to put the beam high enough.

Having the two boys, Espen, five, and Eivind, two, scurrying around on the hillside, losing my pliers, pushing each other off the big rock, oblivious to the play potential of a nifty swing set, wasn't much help, either.

And while they got to watch the Garfield special, I was laboring beneath a cloud of mosquitoes to create a back yard masterpiece out of treated wood and pole-barn nails.

That night, though, I was sure I had enough of the proper materials to get at least one of the swings on properly.

I walked in the back door and plopped the bag of bolts and the swing-set seat and rope onto the kitchen counter.

"Well, I got the stuff," I said to no one in particular, hoping that someone would ask me "what stuff?"

"Yep, got a swing-set seat in there," I said, patting the paper bag.

Suddenly, Espen's head popped up over the counter to eyeball the package.

"What do you have in there, Poppa?" he asked.

Ah, a bite.

"A swing-set seat; We're going to put that baby up tonight," I answered.

Espen had been longing for a swing set. There is a house at the end of the block that has a fancy swing set with a slide and rings and climbing ramp. It is tantalizingly close to the corner of the road where we walk, and we were among the interested neighbors who watched when the dad in that house put the swing set together.

So that night, in the kitchen, with the equipment on the counter, Espen looked up and asked:

"Would you be needing a big boy to help you put that together?"

"I suppose I might," I answered.

"Well then you should know you have a big boy right here," he said, quite seriously.

"That's great. I'm going to need your help," I said. I gave his mother a glance and we smiled.

Eivind came over to investigate why he was not the center of attention.

"I'm a big boy, too," he piped. (Out of diapers for two months now, he will show his Snoopy underpants to anyone who asks and some who don't.)

"So, you are? Then I suppose you can help, too," I said.

After dinner, they got to hand me my pliers and hold up the seat, and climb up the first two rungs of the ladder. The seat looked fine, though I had somehow miscalculated, leaving the seat about three feet off the ground with no way to lengthen the ropes. But everyone got boosts up to the seat, and two nights and one more trip to the lumber yard later, our back yard had a homemade set of two swings attached to a beam strung between two walnut trees. Not exactly the Taj, but it worked and the boys use it.

I have a friend who once, a couple of years ago, insisted that people have children because of the parents' need for unconditional love.

I responded that no love, even the love from a child, is unconditional.

It is based on such things as swing sets and an acknowledgment that yes, I am aware there is a big boy or two big boys around to help me.

And, I am aware that sometimes it is important for me to point out that I could use the help.　　　　　■ **June 1, 1989**

Father's Day
A Day of Rest? Yeah, Sure

I'm taking Father's Day off today.

I'll probably sleep until 6 or 6:30 a.m., get up, make coffee, bring in the paper, feed the cats, then sit on the back porch and read the funnies.

Then Espen, five, will wake up and I'll nag him to put on his slippers.

Then Eivind, two, will wake up and I'll change his overnight diaper, get him to sit on the potty chair and then put a pair of big-boy underpants on him and send him on his way.

Then Else, thirty-something, will wake up.

Then I'll start thinking about making breakfast. Fruit and cereal is what we usually have these days. I'll get out the boys' vitamins and fluoride tablets. I'll see if there is orange juice and if there is none, get some out of the freezer. I'll make sure Espen gets Espen's cereal bowl with the teddy bear on it and Eivind gets Eivind's cereal bowl with the juggling clown on it.

I'll make sure the milk pitcher is half-full, so the boys can pour their own milk without spilling it and we can cluck about how big they are, being able to pour their own milk.

Else and I may talk about how much money is left in the checkbook.

I'll clean up the spilled milk.

Then it will be time to read the Sunday classifieds and see what the family car is worth.

Eivind is now big enough to take over Espen's tricycle, and Espen is big enough for his own two-wheeler. We've been saving our aluminum cans to help pay for a two-wheeler, so we're looking for bicycles, too.

Then I'll read the ad inserts for driveway blacktop sealer deals. It's that time of the year, too. Get the scissors and clip the coupons.

It looks like a busy day, so on this morning I'm taking it easy, I will probably change the oil in my car.

And the garden should be weeded, especially around the tomatoes and the peas. I should probably hill the potatoes this weekend, too, even though they haven't blossomed yet. I'll think of blossoms and remind myself to show the boys the blossoms on their cucumber plants.

As today's breakfast ends, I will rinse the dishes and fill the dishwasher.

Did I mention the vacuuming?

Did anyone see the clothes I was folding?

The bottom porch step is spongy, and I suppose it should be replaced or renailed today, too. The whole deck should be painted, really, but not today.

If it's not blowing out today, I might spray the doorways and sills with insecticide. How do the ants get in here, anyway? And, speaking of insects, the boys' homemade butterfly net needs new cheesecloth. And, speaking of insects, I should de-fog the attic for wasps, too.

Actually, while I'm taking it easy and it's not overly hot out, the woodstove chimney needs a cleaning, and while I'm up there I suppose I could caulk around the flashing. And, while I'm still up there, the eaves' troughs should be cleaned.

The dehumidifier should be rolled out of the laundry room today, too. And the shelves I took down when I painted the basement last summer should be put up again, somewhere. And didn't we talk about putting a couple of storage cubes next to Eivind's bed?

I wonder how many times I will interrupt a sibling argument today with the words: "If you can't share it, nobody's going to play with it."

I wonder how many times I will tie shoelaces, how many times I will count to 10 under my breath, how many times I will forget to count to 10, how many times I will say "move it or lose it, dudes."

Sooner or later today, we may all pile into the station wagon and drive someplace, anyplace.

When we get out of the car, I will say "watch out for cars," and I will put myself between the boys and the traffic.

Tonight, I may help give the outlaws a bath, jumping into the tub myself when they're done.

Not all of this will get done, of course. I will be the last person in the house to fall asleep. At 11 p.m. or so, I may even sneak out the sliding doors to sit in the lawn chair, in my underpants and T-shirt, looking out into the dark, doing what a father rarely gets a chance to do: worry about absolutely nothing at all.

■ **June 18, 1989**

Salad Days: Can Optimist Win Out Over Pepper Factor?

These are Venison and Velveeta Days, two foods I rarely get to taste while we eat as a family.

"Eat the perishables," my wife said lovingly, before leaving with the boys to visit her parents.

Now, they are away, I dig deep in the freezer to find the venison steaks and roasts my brother gave me last fall. I am the only one in this house who likes venison, and everyone else prefers real cheese to processed cheese.

If I work it right, I can have venison steak sandwiches with Velveeta cheese on whole wheat bread for dinner every day while the gang is on vacation.

It won't work, just like my other summer eating plan didn't work. I was going to be self-supplying this summer, eating fresh, crisp salad every day from my leafy garden. After abandoning my big vegetable garden at the bottom of the hill two years ago, this summer I planted a small table-salad vegetable garden in the back yard.

I hauled in some black dirt. I planted: nine tomato plants, six pepper plants, four short rows of radishes and carrots (in the same row), two rows of lettuce, a corner of snap peas and two marigolds on another corner. The boys, Espen and Eivind, planted the three cucumber plants they grew in the rec room last winter and spring.

I mulched, I sprinkled, I dusted, I even bragged for a while when everything seemed to be growing at once.

Also, next to the woodpile, partly in the shade, I planted five short rows of potatoes (five plants in each row). This I did because it was the only place to plant them and because a guy at the office gave me some hotshot seed potatoes. I also planted three potatoes in the front yard, next to the garage.

The take so far: Enough lettuce to make about seven salads, one pepper, seven peas, one cucumber, 35 radishes, one (that's right, just one) tomato.

That's it.

The walnut trees have wiped out the tomatoes. I had hoped bringing in some black dirt would negate the effect of the walnut root juice, but it didn't. The tomatoes grew like crazy for six weeks, looked strong and healthy. But now they are all dead or dying, same as last year.

The peas ignored the elaborate string fence I erected and took a powder early. I suspect the age of the seeds (three years) was a factor. The fence still looks great, though.

There are some salvageable greens. The peppers look good and are blossoming. A second crop of buttercup lettuce is looking so healthy I am working on a response to anyone who might accuse me of buying it at the market and replanting it.

Planting the potatoes next to the woodpile was not, it seems, a great idea. The open space was also previously occupied by a woodpile, and apparently a number of burrowing creatures were accustomed to traveling in tunnels beneath the pile. Planting potatoes there was like planting them in the middle of Interstate 90. They grew, but when I tried to water the plants, the water just disappeared down little holes that appeared between the rows.

So that at least leaves me with some lettuce for my venison steak and Velveeta cheese sandwiches.

And olives. Our refrigerator door is home to three or four half-filled olive jars.

And peppers. Two years ago I bought a half-bushel of peppers after reading one of those food-page features about how easy it is to freeze chopped-up peppers and then have them for use, fresh and crisp, at any time during the year.

The result was a bunch of little baggies filled with chopped-up peppers that, every time we need peppers, is forgotten. (Of course, this is the year the peppers look like they will be the only survivors in my garden.) So the frozen peppers are piled up in the freezer right next to those frozen chives, which came from another food-page feature advising to chop chives, add to water and then freeze in ice cube trays. After frozen, simply put them in baggies and keep in freezer. Whenever you need some fresh chives, thaw out an ice cube.

That works fine, except for the frozen pepper factor.

So, here's to vacation fare: Velveeta, venison steak, buttercup lettuce, olives, chopped peppers and chives.

It's possible, too, that a green tomato on the dead tomato plants will ripen, in which case I will probably quickly freeze it and put it into a plastic bag. ■ **July 23, 1989**

Weekend Landscaping Not a Washout

*A*t 5:15 a.m. Monday, I heard the rain starting and I woke up and went to the garage to salvage my weekend.

Thanks to Sears, K Mart, a disposable diaper, a plastic mattress bag and a shredded woodpile tarp, I succeeded.

This was the weekend I became a landscape artist, transforming a simple 10-foot front-yard slope and eight 8-foot treated logs into a terraced marvel of intricately woven timbers that nestle, even cuddle, an inviting mound of mulch and assorted plants that weed themselves, blossom on demand and repel band-candy saleskids.

The strategy is simple: Buy the timbers, dig up the slope next to the front steps, cut the timbers to fit, tie strings to three stakes so that everything is straight, don't step on the potentillas already growing too close to the steps. Arrange the timbers in a terrace that is about 10 feet long and 5 feet high.

I started to dig up the slope, then discovered that three inches beneath the surface of my front lawn is a hard-packed bed of clay and rocks. I used a spud I bought at my grandmother's auction to chisel out a channel for the timbers.

I bought the timbers, then discovered my shoulder would not push the saw through wet, treated timbers.

So, with only a few feet of work done, I quit Saturday night, intent on buying a chain saw Sunday.

Going through the Sunday ad inserts, I found a chain saw on sale at Sears and topsoil on sale at K Mart. The topsoil would be incentive to finish the project, I thought.

At K Mart, the woman said the shipment of topsoil on sale had not arrived, but "might be here next week."

At Sears, the man said the shipment of chain saws on sale had not arrived, but "might be here some time."

By the time I got home, I was frustrated enough to mow the lawn without stomping down the mole channels, a forgotten task that left my mower hubdeep in several unstomped corners of the back yard.

Then I got out the circular saw and started mistreating the timbers. I had to make two cuts, one on the top and one on the bottom, to go all the way through.

By suppertime Sunday, I was finished. I dug all the old rocky clay out of the hillside, which now sported a carefully framed hole with four potentillas clinging to the side next to the steps. The plan was to dig them up, move them over, then fill it all in with good topsoil.

But with no topsoil, I just left it as it was, drank three Diet Cokes and two quarts of water, put my tools away and then admired the pile of timbers from all possible angles. I wheedled a couple of compliments about it from my wife, took a shower and, as ex-colleague Paul Rix used to say, slept like a dead pig.

Until 5:15 a.m.

That was when the rain started and I woke up, alert to the possibility that my entire weekend's work was about to go floating across my driveway. With the hole unfilled and unmulched, the timbers were exposed and the slope uncovered. The potentillas would follow the timbers and mud, the concrete steps would sink, the house foundation would tip and the floors would pull apart and everyone would have to spit sideways into the bathroom sink when they brushed their teeth.

Fortunately, five years ago I saved a large plastic bag that had protected a new mattress. Some day, I thought, folding it and putting it on a garage shelf, this will come in handy. Monday morning it did.

Barefoot, bare-chested and half-asleep, I found it immediately, along with an old blue tarp—the kind that is shredproof with rustproof grommets—that has rusted grommets and is partly shredded.

In less time than it takes to clip the toenails of a cat, I had the slope covered and I was back in bed, smug and wet.

And the disposable diaper?

Like most parents, I keep a disposable diaper in my car's glove compartment. This was handy Monday morning when I found the car window open.

Absorbent side down, the diaper did a good job of soaking up the rain on my car seat. ■ **August 29, 1989**

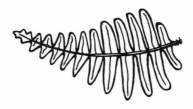

Imagine That . . . We'll Just Dream On

My son Espen was explaining what happened to his shoe-laces on a day-care class trip to a cave.

"They turned out the lights and my shoelaces lighted up," he said.

"You're kidding," I said.

"No," he answered with a slow solemnity that made me lean forward to catch what he was going to say next.

"No, this is for real, Poppa, no kidding," he said.

It is nice that he lets me know when he is talking about things that really happen.

Occasionally, we—that is, Espen, myself and my other son, Eivind—slip into a fantasy world governed by a sort of false reasoning dependent on ways justifying means. So, bunny rabbits don't wear glasses because they eat carrots, and toys left on the living room floor overnight sometimes move themselves into a pile next to the wastebasket because they feel unwanted. Everything may be fantasy, but I put in simplistic cause-effect examples.

I'm not worried this will warp the boys.

For the past two years, Espen has had an imaginary friend he calls Mister Magic Dinosaur. Mister Magic Dinosaur disappeared over the summer, but showed up again in conversations after school started. Eivind has picked up on this and now joins in, though I suspect he is simply doing a three-year-old's version of name-dropping.

I'm not too worried about this fantasy, either. So far, Mister Magic Dinosaur is a sort of flying good-deed-doer, able to appear and reappear as need be, equipped with sophisticated laser claws and other stuff, when necessary. On some days he has parents, the Momma Mister Magic Dinosaur and the Poppa Mister Magic Dinosaur, and he tends to show up in the nick of time or sometimes he just shows off his unusual powers.

The other fantasies are manifested in made-up bedtime stories and such activities as moose bites.

Our particular moose bite tradition comes from Tom Reiter, a former neighbor who gave his kids, and other people's kids, moose bites by forming a "C" with his hand and, placing the clamp right above the knee, giving a firm, wide, but gentle pinch and yelling "MOOSE BITE, MOOSE BITE."

Our version requires the biter to divert the attention of the bitee, usually by pointing to another direction and saying, "Hey, look at that giraffe over there."

When the bitee looks, the biter administers the moose bite.

There is no giraffe, of course, and this is not a real moose bite, of course, but it always gets a big laugh. I don't think *Psychology Today* will send a reporter out to analyze this.

We used to pick up our boys, when they were babies, and place them tummy down on top of our heads and yell "Baby Hat, Baby Hat." This was always good for a laugh, and I do it once in a while now, too, and it is still good for a laugh.

But, it seems, even five-year-olds want to get back to real life once in a while. Saturday-morning and late-afternoon cartoons hold great interest for Espen and Eivind, but I can draw both sons away from the television simply by finding a toad in a flower bed. There may be invincible Ninja Turtles on the tube, but it is far more fun to investigate a squashed toad in the driveway.

Reality over fantasy, in that case.

Where will this fantasy stop?

I'm hoping it doesn't stop, in some ways, since it hasn't stopped for me. I'm a firm believer in promoting fantasy as an incentive for improving reality.

Would I, as a boy, have spent hours chasing crazy caroms of a rubber ball bounced off our front concrete steps if I did not fantasize I would someday be playing for the high school varsity team, or even the Braves in Milwaukee?

Is there a writer in this business who does not carry around a gem of an idea for a breakthrough novel?

I've discovered I'm a willing participant, even instigator, in all this fantasy/reality mixing. Mostly, it all starts with a question.

Espen will ask: "You know what?"

And I say: "No, what?"

And he explains, as he did last week, that "really, Mister Magic Dinosaur is only in my wonder."

"In your wonder?" I ask.

"Yah, in my wonder. He's not for real. I wonder him," he said.

"Ahh, I get it," I say, pondering and envying his wonder.

Meanwhile, the little brother is asking another question:

"Hey, Poppa, you know what I can do?"

And I say: "No, what?"

And he stands on one leg in the middle of the driveway and uses his other leg to give a push and he twirls around.

"See, I can dance."

"I see."

Hah, a cynic would say. In your dreams.

So far, I would answer. So far.　　　　■ **September 24, 1989**

Knock-knock Jokes Have Me Going Bananas

haven't noticed the child-rearing experts keeping track of this yet, so I thought I would be first out with it. Has anyone else noted the dreadful lack of knock-knock joke education? (Banana) Is it Nintendo's fault? Can knock-knock jokes be responsible for moving our society further toward cultural impotence in our schools? (Banana who?) Is it because knock-knock jokes do not make fun of ethnic groups or minorities? (Banana) I walked around the office one day recently and solicited knock-knock jokes and didn't get one new one. (Banana who?) My sons have more options in Ghostbuster action figures than they do in knock-knock jokes. (Orange) (And, why are they called "action" figures? They don't do anything. I've seen more action in a leisure suit on State Street.) I love it when my kids tell jokes. The boys have the idea, but not the punchline. (Orange who?) Here is a typical meatloaf dinner joke: Espen, squeezing the equivalent of 17 tomatoes worth of ketchup on to his meatloaf: Hear me. Hear me. Wanna hear a joke?

Me: Okay. That's enough ketchup.

Espen: Ready?

Me: Ready. Let's hear it. Hey, no more ketchup.

Espen: Why did the, ah, worm, (giggle) cross the road?

Me: I don't know. Why did the worm cross the road?

Espen: Dirt. Yah, hah hah.

This punchline is followed by gales of laughter, Else and I smack our foreheads in delirium, Eivind (the three-year-old) yells "Dirt, Hah, Worm, Hah, Road, Hah," and Espen eventually leans back, basking in the attention, ketchup dripping from his sleeves.

(Orange you glad I didn't say Banana?) See. Everyone knows the Banana-Orange knock-knock joke. Now my sons know it, but of course they say it backward every time they try to tell it. Which makes it even funnier. Try ending that joke with Banana-who.

Both boys know the salmon knock-knock joke. (Salmon who? Salmon chanted evening.) Once they get the tune right, they will wander the hallways singing "Salmon Chanted EEEEEEEVening" for 30 minutes, stopping only to fall down laughing.

And my father just told them the highway cop knock-knock joke. (Highway cop who? Highway cop about seven each morning.) We even have made their names into knock-knock jokes:

Espen who? Espen nice talking to you.

Eivind who? Eivind looking for a good place to park my car.

We have recently progressed to the old Banana-In-My-Ear routine, which both boys find hilarious. (First man: Say, did you know you have a banana in your ear? Second man: I'm sorry, I can't hear you, I have a banana in my ear.) As I have many times said: This fatherhood is a tough gig, but the home crowds are easy to please.   ■ **December 3, 1989**

Keeping the Fabric From Unraveling

At about 10 a.m. today, my wife will direct dial her parents in Eidanger, Norway, to say Merry Christmas. They will have already eaten a traditional Christmas Eve dinner, and they—probably including my wife's sister, her husband, and my wife's aunt—will be waiting for the call.

One by one they will come to the phone to say a few words, ask about the weather. Nothing the newspapers would consider worthy of follow-up will be discussed. The conversations will be uneven because of the split-second difference in timing that overseas calls seem to have, and because, even though everyone knows the call is coming, no one ever really prepares for it.

The call has become a Christmas tradition.

My boys will get to talk to Moo-moo and Moo-fah (mother's mother and mother's father), but mostly my wife will catch up on local gossip and make sure everyone is healthy. The point is not what is said, really, but that the call is made, that something is said, something is done to keep the fabric of the family from unraveling.

I suspect it is the same with Christmas cards.

We don't send long letters with Christmas cards. Just a few words jotted with a felt-tip pen on the back of a rare photograph of our two sons standing still. A few of my friends in faraway places (Minneapolis, to name one) have taken to word-processing a long missive. It is not something I would do, but I enjoy reading them and imagining the editing process.

I just heard from an old friend who, in her mass-produced letter, placed in a Christmas card, noted that she, on only four days notice, arranged a spur-of-the-moment four-week trip for herself to South America, the Amazon and similar points while her husband went on a business trip to Asia (seven countries in eight days).

It should come as no surprise that this couple has no children.

The odd part of the mass-produced letter, though, was that on the back of that letter she had a full-page hand-written letter filled with the kind of chatty comments, interesting requests and out-of-world plans that made her a dear friend in the first place.

We have not spoken to each other in several years, but our Christmas cards are what pass for continuing a friendship, a way of keeping something from unraveling.

Several years ago, when my grandmother was in her 80s, I showed up unannounced at the door of her Rockland home. We sat in her kitchen, drank coffee and ate molasses cookies while she talked, with only a bit of questioning from me. She talked into a microphone and her memories were recorded. She told stories of hardship and harmony, of growing up in the coulees and ridges of La Crosse and Monroe counties, of big families, of presents of handkerchiefs, of her children.

She died in February 1984. For Christmas 1986, I made several copies of the tape of her conversations and sent them as a surprise to my father, and aunts and uncles.

I don't do this often, but sometimes I will sit in the darkened living room of our home, turn on the tape deck and listen to my grandmother talk.

I already know what she is going to say. Listening is a way of keeping in touch, too. ■ **December 24, 1989**

Hesselberg Knows Hockey? Well... Maybe

*O*ne day recently Eivind and I were moping around the garage, looking for something to do.

Espen was too busy creating Lego booby traps through the hall and beneath the bunk beds to join us.

It was warm enough to open the garage door but cold enough that mittens, scarves and boots were necessary. Eivind also had on snow pants, which are not so much to protect against snow as to pad the knees and rump for the inevitable falls and stumbles.

I had already shown him how to use the Shop-Vac, so that was no fun any more.

In one corner of the garage, against the wall, we found my old hockey stick. At least 20 years old, it is a simple wooden hockey stick, no curves, no replaceable blade, just a stick.

Eivind saw it, wanted it and, being my son, had no idea what to do with it when he got it.

The stick is about twice as long as he is, but he grabbed it in the middle after I showed him how to swoosh it along the asphalt.

In a few minutes he had mashed all the snow clumps left on the driveway, so I dug into the recycling bin and pulled out a "I Can't Believe It's Not Butter" container.

Eivind slammed that around for a while and had a great time, bonking himself on the head and poking himself in the tummy with the butt end of the stick every other shot.

I attempted to stop the action to tell a story, something I do to prove to my boys that I was a kid once, too. He didn't listen—which I'm told is a trait of hockey players in general—but here's the story I was trying to tell.

This hockey stick, I said, is the only hockey stick I ever owned and it was used when I was a ringer for a UW-Madison fraternity 20 years ago, in the winter of 1969-70.

I lived in the Lakeshore dorms that freshman year, but a friend was a frat rat and they needed hockey players, so I joined the team for one game.

I learned how to play hockey at Dead River (a swamp, really, off the La Crosse River between Rockland and Sparta) and at the Weldon Pond in Bangor. Dead River was a great place to learn the game since there were raw hockey sticks all over the place, thanks to dead trees. At the end of a game of hockey on a cold afternoon, we'd burn the sticks.

We ice skated every night and weekend through the winter— at night we went to the VFW rink in the park, where they had lights, music and the Althoff and Stratman girls, and also we skated up Dutch Creek, just to show off—until we were old enough to play basketball, or what our coach called a "real sport."

I'm not sure when or where I got the hockey stick, but I had it when I drove with Dan Jones and six other guys in a VW bug to a fraternity hockey game. In the locker room, all my teammates were taping Life magazines around their legs. It is true that when I walked in, they had to find a pair of Time magazines for me.

It was a terrible game. I hadn't learned any rules while playing hockey on Dead River, and I wasn't used to a real hockey stick and, then there was the idea of using a real puck and, playing indoors, well, I guess it was all the glamour. I stunk up the rink.

We lost by double figures and drank a lot of beer at Shakey's on East Washington Avenue afterward. I didn't know the words to the dirty songs the guys were singing and I never played hockey again.

Not, that is, until a couple weeks ago, when Eivind and I mixed it up on the driveway, me with a tree branch and he with a hockey stick, lifting into the air a plastic margarine cup and me hollering GOAL GOAL GOAL.

Next year maybe we'll look for a swamp and burn a couple of sticks. I love growing up again.　　　　■ **March 6, 1990**

Bike 'Class' Has Lesson for Teacher

There is no book on parenthood with a chapter about Teaching Your Child to Ride a Bicycle.

If there was, I would ignore it on principle, just as I have ignored all child-rearing books except Dr. Spock (the baby guy, not the Star Trek guy).

Espen is six and it's high time he learned how to ride his two-wheeler without the training wheels.

He bought it himself last summer with aluminum can money. The deal was he paid half and I paid half and we got a nice one, though it has no fenders. Most bikes these days have no fenders, a sure sign that this is the T-shirt age, or the age when kids don't ride bikes in the rain.

So we got a red bike without fenders. It has knobby wheels and we put glow-in-the-dark doodads on the spokes and there is a bell.

All last summer he was able to roll back and forth on the driveway, with the help of training wheels. Sometimes he would take his show on the road, going along on his "four-wheeler" bicycle, while little brother Eivind rode his tricycle, on our walks around the neighborhood.

But Espen's friends Teddy and Kevin have bicycles too, and they can ride them. Teddy lives in town and Kevin lives just up the street. It is impossible for a boy on a bike with training wheels to ride as fast as a boy on a bike without training wheels.

It was important—to me it was important—that Espen and Kevin be able to bicycle around the block together, to race one another, to zoom into and out of ditches.

They are just now getting to know each other, sort of hanging out in a non hanging-out sort of way. The sort of hanging out that comes about without appointment, where a kid will see another kid and just, well, hang out, picking up sticks or goofing off in the sandbox or collecting ladybugs, bouncing the superball onto the roof, or going back and forth on the swingseats on your belly together, not really talking but saying "hey" and "c'mon" and "no way, man." That sort of thing.

It hurt my heart when I first saw Espen abandon his bicycle along the road because he couldn't keep up. How does he feel, I wondered, watching his friend ride away. I got the idea he didn't want to take his bicycle on our walks anymore. I felt terrible.

So I removed the training wheels and told Espen it was easy as pie just let me hold you up and you pedal like crazy.

That's not the way, we learned. I got too mad too easily. It was supposed to be as simple as riding a bike.

But it's not that simple. It's balance and speed and learning to get on and off and mostly, patience.

I didn't learn that until one night, frustrated by Espen's lack of enthusiasm, I took him and the bicycle to a big empty flat parking lot.

I gave him a push and he pedaled for about 10 yards. But he didn't steer and I got mad because he seemed to be ignoring my expert instructions.

"How many times do I have to tell you . . ." is the way I started, ready to give it another go.

But he didn't want to continue. I had scared him and, with that, scared myself. I could read his face, which said he was afraid of something and I figured it was me.

Just to ride a bike, I had scared my son.

I gave him the kind of hug a father gives when the father knows he has done wrong. A guilt hug, I guess. My motives were pure but my methods were stupid.

I tossed the bike in the back seat.

I told Espen that riding a bike was not a big deal and that sooner or later, when he felt like it, we would try it again.

And now every night we make a couple runs from the end of the driveway to the lawn at the side of the house, a slight slope and softer than a parking lot. He can do it, all by himself if I give him a good push at the start.

If he wants, he can pedal farther back behind the house, and by now he is getting pretty good at it. Not enough to join Kevin yet, slamming on the brakes and sliding around corners.

But enough. Just enough to have a little success, to get confident.

He's a good teacher, too.

In his six years, this is the seventh or eighth time he has given me a good lesson in patience.　　　　■ **June 3, 1990**

How Dumb Do They Think We Are?

They Must Think We're Really Dumb

Once in a great while in this business, you come into contact with The Best. Simply, there is none better. Imagine then, not one, but two candidates for the best in this edition of How Dumb Do They Think We Are, the ongoing exposure of attempts to sell something you don't need, at a price you can't afford, from someone you shouldn't trust.

The cream of this crop has to be the post card from "Cartwig, Chandler-Jones and Smyth," of New York City. On the front is printed: "An anonymous donor has given me the task of finding you. If you are the right person all I can tell you is that 10 million dollars could be yours."

The name itself (Smyth?) is worthy of mention. We hicks in Wisconsin are supposed to be impressed by that. And this card is signed by none other than "Prescott Winton, for the firm of Cartwig . . ."

Prescott Winton, a nom de scam if ever there was one, writes that he is looking for the person whose name is on the card.

"To establish your identity beyond a shadow of a doubt, I shall require a sample of your handwriting plus your legal signature. Further, you must send me a check for $20 to do the computer search, compare your handwriting and file the papers required by the anonymous donor."

How will Prescott Winton consummate this deal?

"I will deposit your check and send you the winning lottery numbers an anonymous donor has put aside for you. All I'm permitted to say at this time is that these winning lottery numbers could be worth more than 10 million dollars to you."

The receiver, to supply a handwriting sample, has to write: "Here is $20. I am the person you are looking for."

This qualifies for the HDDTTWA WAH (What a Hoot) prize, which must be shared with the "Department of Sweepstakes Administration, Sweepstakes Annex Tower 8th Floor, Canton, Ohio."

Joe Lasch of Lake Mills has latched on to this classic. He has won a "flawless, one carat, 58 sparkling facet, hand cut and polished Lindenwold Cubic Zirconia CZ Diamond simulant." This "simulant," of course, comes with a Certificate of Authenticity. In other words, it's an authentic fake diamond.

Not only that, the Sweepstakes Administration Department has used its influence to get Lasch a bargain of 50 to 80 percent off in mounting that diamond in a "tiffany ring," "lavish pendant," "formal earrings" or a "handsome gentlemen's ring or tie tac." This gets better. The form for ordering those mountings puts the value of the jewelry as between $1,600 and $3,200, but if you look for the asterisk, you find that these values are only "comparable jewelers cost using a mined diamond."

And so the cost to Lasch is only between $19 and $69, the mounting fee.

Lasch, however, wisely ignored the testimonial paragraph from Zsa Zsa Gabor and let this ring deal slip through his fingers.

And, in keeping up with old dodges, Chrysler Corp. has yet to send checks to consumers affected in the disconnected odometer case, supposedly settled more than 14 months ago.

Chrysler settled with officials in 45 states following charges that two company employees conspired to sell more than 60,000 vehicles whose odometers were disconnected while they were driven by Chrysler officials.

Consumers who bought the vehicles were supposed to receive $500 each, but many say they haven't even received claim forms.

Also, ignore, unless you want to buy a $398.25 filter for your kitchen faucet, the shamelessly bogus come-on from Q.W.S. which begins with "I have tried to contact you . . ."

This sort of surprise introduction is showing up too often. For the record, Q.W.S. stands for Quality Water Systems.

River Bend Resort, one of my favorite originators of HDDTTWA mail, has another howler in the post. This one is routed through Fairway Courier Service, which uses a transparently false "Return Notice" in the form of a shipping invoice.

What this is, is the chance to tour beautiful River Bend Resort and claim "TWO stated prizes." The notice also says that "you are definitely a cash award recipient." This is exciting until you read the fine print, which notes that the "cash award" is really a $5 gasoline allowance.

What's a HDDTTWA column without an update on Madam Daudet, the Hackensack seer who keeps promising to help me win the lottery? Well, *c'est fini, madame,* because here comes Mrs. Michelle Dumont, who has psychically tracked down thousands of Wisconsin residents "who are worried."

Dumont predicts an upcoming five-month "brilliant period." She will, for $17.90, send each person she has had psychic vibrations about a personal "golden number" and eight charts to be used for the lottery, horse racing, professional success and love.

Wooooo. It's working already. I just saved $17.90.

■ **April 2, 1989**

Most of Us Have Been En-list-ed

T oo obvious. No one would ever buy a double cheese-burger at McDonald's for $1.74 plus tax instead of two single cheeseburgers at 82¢ each.

And who would think that the $1.74 price of a salad at Kohl's did not include the tiny packet of salad dressing, which costs 23¢ extra?

Hah, no one ever went broke—or hungry, come to think of it— underestimating the American public's appetitite for getting less for more.

And the crack investigative staff that infrequently, but incessantly and always politely, asks How Dumb Do They Think We Are? is back in the loop. The HDDTTWA movement, begun from anonymous tips about chain-letter pyramid schemes collected in a second-hand manilla folder inexplicably labeled "SNAKE LADY," rises once again to scrutinize the inscrutables and deflate the inflatables.

To do so, this past month HDDTTWA infiltrated the Advon Mailing Lists company, of Shelly, Idaho, by calling and asking for a price list.

There is no fleece without a mailing list, and here is where many shearers get theirs. Advon offers names in four categories: "Less than 45-day-old opportunity seekers, 1,000 names for $40," or "Multi-level prospects, 1,000 names for $50," or "Home Business Opportunity Seekers, 1,000 names for $45," or "Over

45-day-old opportunity Seekers, 1,000 names for $25."

Advon's rate list goes up to 100,000 names, for $1,500. Chances are good yours is one of those "rented."

(In mailing list jargon, by the way, a "Nixie" is an address provided but returned as undeliverable.)

They can rent you names from 25 categories, including "Religious Product Buyers," and, of course "Mailing List Buyers."

In a perfect world, the only list would be the list of list buyers and they could pyramid each other into oblivion.

And in a perfect world, HDDTTWA would not have to warn people about the credit-card application from American TV and Appliance that requires the applicant to provide a Social Security number. There is no need to do this, a credit card company has no need for your Social Security number, though clearly they will use it to gather credit information from a credit bureau. Paranoids need not apply, and that includes most of the members of the HDDTTWA staff.

Thanks to HDDTTWA reader Douglas Dillman, who mistakenly paid his subscription twice to Car and Driver magazine. He thinks magazines send and send again invoices on purpose, and that is why the invoices never include information on the subscription period.

"Assume a company publishes several magazines with a total circulation of 50 million, with an average yearly subscription rate of $15. Further suppose the practice induces 2 percent of all subscribers to double-pay. Such a practice would bring in $15 million in additional undeserved revenue per year," calculates Dillman.

Dillman suggested that HDDTTWA try to catch the magazines at this by paying a subscription promptly, then paying again when the next invoice shows up, then waiting for the magazine to discover the double payment and refund the money. Really, HDDTTWA?

The Gibson-Homans Company of Twinsburg, Ohio, knows. They sell Shur-stik, a "siliconized acrylic caulk" and they sold a tube of the stuff to Ronald Calkins, of Mazomanie.

Calkins noted that the caulk is a "35-year warranty" caulk, but that to get a rebate (expires June 30) on the caulk he has to destroy the tube by cutting out the product code. He made a photocopy of the tube and sent that, with a letter explaining the dilemma. No word of his rebate yet.

And the latest mailings from USA Wholesale, Fort Lauderdale, Fla., is out. They send a notice that a "Singer Sewing Machine has arrived at our distribution center and is now available for immediate shipment to you," at a cost of only $24.97. The machine is the "compact model-x50B."

This is an old one, where the truth is misleading. That "compact" Singer is really a hand-held, toy-type stitcher. It is a Singer, and it is a sewing machine, and it is worth a lot less than $24.97.

The HDDTTWA's Chain Letter of the Month is the Zerox Clown Collection, apparently the plan of J.A. McCarthy of Glen Burnie, Md. He has an unlisted telephone number, but I have three "Zerox" copies of clowns being mailed around, suggesting people send him $2 and a clown.

I wonder how you get on a clown mailing list?

The final word from HDDTTWA is supplied by the advertisement for the "NEW! Small Pads! SOS Juniors" The ad promoting the new "compact steel wool soap pads" reads "A Fresh Pad Every Day . . . No Waste!"

No waste? A fresh pad every day?   ■ **June 10, 1990**

See Gulls?
Things Are Fishy Here

Is there a sign, written in code perhaps, at the Illinois border to Wisconsin?

"Welcome, unethical, dishonest and worthless pups, dregs of the con-artist barrel, escapers of ethics. Welcome to Wisconsin, You're Among Gulls."

Or maybe the message is sent by mind travel to all the mail-order hucksters in their cloned strip-mall suites in the patron state of telecommunication hustling, Florida.

Whatever. It's Spring. The pyramid chain letters are in the mail, and the staff of the How Dumb Do They Think We Are (HDDTTWA)—dedicated to rending the rotting fabric of capitalism's lowest denominators—is on duty.

■ First, a tip of the mail box flap to those pesky charge-card companies that insist on charging for a gift.

"Our Gift To You . . ." reads the intro to the flier stuffed in Master Charge statements earlier this year.

"After the holiday spending, your budget could probably use a lift. So you're invited to skip the January payment on your MasterCard. Take advantage of this great way to begin 1990."

Thanks, but no thanks. At least the notice, in tiny letters, explains that finance charges continue to add up.

■ In a special HDDTTWA WAH (What A Hoot) nomination, Cash World of Las Vegas papered the state with atypical "Return This Card and Collect Your Prize" post cards on which the gull only has to "Solve puzzle and you win!"

In three rows of words, the contest entrant must pick out the word that doesn't belong with the rest. To appreciate how dumb this really is, consider that in row two, the words are Too, Boo, Goo, Woo, Coo and Runs.

■ More contests? Pity the poor unpublished poet who responds to the American Poetry Association's solicitation (carried in this newspaper, no less) for entries in its "contest."

The association, once the poet has entered, accepts the work for the American Poetry Anthology. Then comes the pitch: If the poet ever wants to read his or her work published, it will cost $40 for the book. And, "for each poem you include, we request that you buy at least one copy of the book," at a cost of $32 for every book after the first.

The anthology is not available—nor should it be—at the Madison Public Library.

■ What list of scams would be complete without someone tapping the Big Person for an endorsement? Don Stewart of Phoenix, sends a tiny pencil and a sheet of paper.

Stewart, after quoting from *Genesis, First* and *Second Kings, John,* and *Deuteronomy,* asks the receiver to "Lay your hands flat on the paper I've enclosed and trace around them."

Then, "give $100, $50 or $25 . . . mail the paper, that has the tracing of your hand, along with the offering." When Don the Evangelist gets the mail, he says, "I will lay my hands on top of the place where you draw your hands, and I will pray that God's blessing of Miracle Prosperity will be released in your life immediately."

I believe I know what Brother Stewart wants to lay his hands on.

■ In other financial news, in a 20-page solicitation for subscribers to his *Wilkerson Report,* sort of financial newsletter "about new lifestyle opportunities," publisher William Bonner emits this math-defying statement: "The U.S. economy has been expanding without pause for eight years. That's the longest peacetime growth spurt in more than half a decade."

■ Before the HDDTTWA runs out of space, the National Law Enforcement Memorial Fund must be mentioned.

The fund-raising letters from this outfit are straight from the worst of the worst, contacting old people who can't afford the donation, using all the old ruses, such as guaranteeing "priority seating" to $15 donors at the dedication ceremony. The memorial may be a good idea, but the fund-raising methods should embarrass every law officer.

■ HDDTTWA? A young woman who bought her first used car at a Madison dealer last year showed me her finance contract: She had no idea she was paying 30 percent interest and the contract had been packed with more than $300 in premiums (also financed) for unnecessary insurance. Never buy a car alone.

■ If you received a come-on from Pase Photography, of Aurora, Ill., seeking photographers, recall please the similar come-on from the Pase Literary Society, also of Aurora, also of Pase Publications, which brought us the "iron-clad $1,000 writing assignment." Answer at your own economic risk.

■ **April 1, 1990**

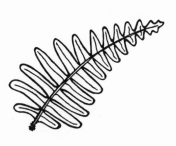

Cereal Box Doesn't Have Total Story

*O*nce, as a callow youth, I believed everything I read.

Now, as chief evidence technician and support staff for the efforts of How Dumb Do They Think We Are, which seeks to expose the soft underbelly of hype to the daggers of public scrutiny (not to mention exaggeration), I spend a fair amount of time reading the unbelievable.

So does Janet Ebsen, of Madison, and all she read was the back of her box of Total Raisin Bran, which provided evidence enough to alert HDDTTWA.

The box says that Total Raisin Bran has "Four Times The Vitamin Nutrition of Kellogg's or Post Raisin Bran." Then, there are three charts for comparison.

In tiny letters, though, it is shown that the nutrition supplies of 1.5 ounces of Total is being compared with the nutrition of only one ounce of Post Raisin Bran and only one-quarter ounce of Kellogg's Raisin Bran. And, the Total and Kellogg's cereals have totals that include the use of fortified (A and D) skim milk, but the milk with the Post cereal is not fortified. If it had been, the Post would have leaped past Total in some nutrition categories.

As Ebsen writes, "Why did Total ever bring up the issue, when any logical, observant consumer can tell they just don't pass muster?"

■ Another addition problem is presented by a company called "USA Refund," which advertises that it "is working for the people," but is really charging money for what is essentially free information.

The ad says it "works with the resources of the U.S. Government to distribute funds that are owed to the public." It does this at a cost of $5 for the first minute and $1 per minute thereafter, plus 10 percent of any refund located.

Though that ad ran in December, the 1-900-number was attached to a different business when I called it this week, and it said it never heard of USA Refund.

Perhaps it went out of business because any citizen can call the government and get the same information for free. For example, the IRS has $47 million from the past three years in undeliverable tax refunds.

The IRS has a toll-free number for its "Tele-Tax System" with that refund information. It is 1-800-554-4477. I called last week, and a recording said no information would be available until after March 1.

■ Another 900-number comes from GHL Hot Line, which offers a $160 "shopping spree coupon" to lucky junk post card receivers and can be claimed for "immediate 30-day delivery" by calling a 900-number, which costs $3.98. Or a lucky winner can return the post card, which requires "hand-sorting and takes up to 12 weeks to process." Gee, here is a company in which "immediate" means 30 days and in which three months are needed to read a post card. Sure, I'd love to order overpriced merchandise from it.

■ Speaking of 900-numbers, I was going to call the television-advertised 1-900-999-LOAN that "absolutely guarantees a loan" to anyone, but the call costs $35 and, according to the small print (captured on Tammy Pompleen's VCR in Evansville), those loan guys don't give out loans; it is simply an information service. And that great advice will cost $35, which will show up on your phone bill. Pompleen said this belongs in the HDDTTWSYFA, or How Dumb Do They Think We Struggling Young Families Are?

■ Struggling Young Families might also want to check their manure meters after reading the mailing from The Leader Corporation, which is selling "High Q" vitamins for children at a cost of $25 for a month's supply. The company says its "High Q" vitamins will not only "give your child a chance to excel in the classroom" but is good for hyperactivity and short attention spans.

The promo also tells parents not to rely on vitamins available (and much cheaper) in pharmacies and stores.

This should be called "Hype Q," and the insidiousness of this is that yes, poor nutrition may affect a child's learning, but that may be more a reflection of poverty than anything else. And poor people certainly cannot afford to pay $25 a month for "Hype Q."

■ Remember the coffee-drinkers-are-more-frequent-lovers survey of last week? Those with longer memories might remember the old mail-order scam that offered high-priced "Bio-Gene 81" sex-pills to old people. Those pills were found to contain, what else, caffeine, and you can expect them back on the market, soon.   ■ **January 28, 1990**

Weather or Not to Believe in Predictions

ne hot day last month — July 11 to be exact — an unemployed spiritualist in Lantana, Fla., mailed letters to 18 cities. One of the cities was Madison.

"I am a spiritualist with an ability to influence weather," the letter began.

"I am writing you to say that I have received a request to end the drought five days after you receive this letter."

I received the letter July 12. It rained 3.5 inches (unofficially) here on July 16.

So I called the spiritualist (on the phone, of course; my mind makes only local calls) in Lantana. He is Jualt Christos.

I got his answering machine (No, the machine did not say "I've been expecting you to call"), and he called me back.

I said we had received rain within three days of receiving his letter. I said thanks for the rain.

He said, you're welcome, and that all 18 cities he had on his influence list received rain within the requisite five days.

He wouldn't say who requested that he intercede on Wisconsin's behalf, but that "some friends of mine down here who had just returned from Wisconsin said you had some bad problems with the drought."

He said that he generally uses his influence on the weather in the Key West area to steer hurricanes away, but that he takes occasional out-of-state requests.

I asked if some people might say his influence and the actual happening might just be coincidence.

"That's all right," he said, adding he is simply using his "God-given" gift in conjunction with science to "align with that which is natural."

He admitted to being able to "steer" existing weather and to studying weather patterns before making predictions.

A lot of skeptics used to ask him to prove himself, said Christos, but he doesn't do those sorts of requests anymore because he's not in it for the money.

"I don't charge for my services," he said, "and that allows me to say no." He claimed a "96-percent success rate."

I admitted to being skeptical about his predictions and influence, but then he brought up the name of James Randi.

Randi, a magician and author, for 24 years has been debunking psychic con artists around the world. He offers $10,000 to anyone who can prove he or she is truly psychic. He still has his $10,000.

Christos claimed to have passed Randi's tests in 1982, getting 31 of 33 of Randi's "requests" correct.

"He never gave me the money, the $10,000. He dropped me like a hot potato," said Christos.

To double-check this claim, I called the Committee for the Scientific Investigation of Claims of the Paranormal, a non-profit scientific and educational organization which publishes the Skeptical Inquirer, one of my favorite publications. They put me in touch with Randi.

"I get this maybe twice a month from reporters calling to check on a psychic who says I won't pay him" the $10,000, said Randi, adding that such claims are "part of the risks you run in this business."

Actually, said Randi, stopping a drought is one of the easier tasks of any spiritualist or psychic.

"It's always going to rain eventually, and you can always take credit for it," he said.

If a spiritualist really could control the weather, perhaps to prove it he should "keep the drought going for six years," Randi said.

Randi said Christos is one of many "rainmakers and cloud-busters" who are "a dime a dozen" and who sincerely believe they have unusual powers.

None of the makers or busters — including Christos — has ever been able to pass an objectively administered test of the power to influence the weather, Randi said.

I know, a bagatelle, really.

Christos says he is now unemployed and he is looking for work as a substitute teacher "in any field."

"If you have a need, just give me a call," he offered.

He added that Jualt Christos is not his real name.

Using a pseudonym "shields us from the kooks," he said.

Christos was quite happy when I told him that it had rained in Wisconsin and the drought ended.

I was getting to like the fellow, so I didn't have the heart to tell him that it had rained on July 9 and 10, too. We got more than an inch of rain that weekend. That would have been at least two days BEFORE Christos even wrote his letter predicting that the drought would end.

What do I think?

I think Christos is a nice guy who is not trying to rip anyone off and who thinks he has powers that he really does not have. I think his predictions are worth exactly what they cost.

■ **August 14, 1989**

It's Psychic: Get the Connection?

It's a jungle, I know.

But thank goodness the mail got through to Jean Keliher, of Madison.

Otherwise she wouldn't have heard from Sister Maria, of the Crystal Complex, New York, N.Y. And then the good sister would never have made top dog in this month's version of How Dumb Do They Think We Are, in which we answer our own redundant question: How Dumb Do They Think We Are (HDDTTWA)?

Oh, sorry. I interrupted the "psychic connection" between Sister Maria and YOUR NAME HERE. Sister Maria wrote because she knows "you have been trying very hard the last few years to break out of the cycle of despair and hard luck that has been dogging you."

She knows "you are very unhappy, and you need money and friends. I know that things are very hard right now and that you have been hoping to win the lottery. I also know that you have not won anything and you have given up believing." Pretty depressing, huh?

Never fear. The sister writes that "in the next 30 days you will be a winner in the lottery."

Now, read this carefully. I am not making this up. This is what Sister Maria wrote:

"I have information for you that could make you a very big

winner, but the psychic connection is not strong enough. I need to hold in my hand something of yours . . . something that you have in your possession. Something that you will hold in your right hand for 10 minutes while you meditate. I SEE IT NOW. Take a $10 bill, hold it in your right hand for 10 minutes. While you are holding it, visualize all the good things you want to come true. Now take that $10 and wrap it in the top part of this letter. The part with the circle and your name and address and send it to me . . . and I will send you the LUCKY LOTTERY numbers I have for you."

Hmmm. I wonder if it's legal to send personal psychic vibrations through the mail.

Having doubts about Sister Maria?

How about Lynne Palmer, astrologer of the stars, of the Palmer Astrology Center, New York?

The Palmer method is available by toll-free telephone number for $20 to anyone who meets her qualifications: You must not earn $100,000 a year or more, and you must not be "any kind of nationally known person or celebrity."

And, because many of Palmer's Hollywood clients "would be angered if they knew I was virtually giving away the same secrets they have paid up to thousands of dollars for," you must sign an "oath of confidentiality."

Unfortunately for me, as a respected member of the news media, I cannot sign the "oath of confidentiality," thus losing out on my Personal Power Numbers and the Special Days and Lucky Numbers, wealth, happiness and "certain success in gambling, romance, business, social situations every day of my life."

Uh oh. I'm getting these psychic vibrations. I see the need to move on to yet another example of HDDTTWA.

It's from the Institute for Lottery Studies, 2071 National Press Building, Washington, D.C. The institute is related—in motive, at least—to the "Department of Sweepstakes Administration, Sweepstakes Annex," in Canton, Ohio, that was included in last month's HDDTTWA.

The institute sent Francis Renz, of Sun Prairie, a congratulations post card informing him of a 95-percent "Guaranteed Win Chance" of a foreign lottery.

Unfortunately, the institute doesn't have a telephone number.

The Justice Department does, though, and passed along a couple reminders about foreign lotteries to Wisconsin consumers. First, it is illegal to purchase lottery tickets through the mail. Next, foreign lottery tickets are sometimes sold by bootleggers at three to four times the original cost. Also, usually they sell only a purchase confirmation. What if you need the winning ticket for proof of purchase (not an unusual request, eh)?

The foreign lottery pitches are big these days. Several readers sent versions of pitches for the "South German State Lottery," the Canada lottery and others.

The South German Lottery promotion, by the way, doesn't say so, but it is actually selling the same ticket up to eight times. That's correct, the so-called "Basic Ticket," guaranteeing a 48-percent chance to win, is really one-eighth of a ticket. It is sold to seven other people, each with an equal chance of winning. But, as one ticket agent told me on the telephone from Florida (where else) last week, it is quite possible that you will win less than the amount you paid for the ticket.

Sounds like a good deal to me. Is this a great country or what? You can lose money in a lottery along the Rhine from the comfort of your own reclining chair. Talk about the melting pot.

■ **May 14, 1989**

UW Libraries Visiting Shoe Thief Identified

For five years, UW-Madison police Detective Herb Hanson has been waiting for the other shoe to drop. Make that shoes, plural.

And they dropped Tuesday, after Hanson interviewed a 33-year-old Iowa man who admitted taking side trips from Dubuque to Madison for five years to steal shoes—mostly penny loafers and deck shoes, sizes 8 to 9-1/2, depending on the brand name—from students at UW-Madison campus libraries.

The man, an assistant professor of business at a small private college, told Hanson he also stole shoes from students using libraries at Illinois State University at Normal and the University of Illinois at Champagne-Urbana.

Hanson would not identify the man, but said he had been convicted of theft in a missing shoe case at Illinois State last July.

A shoe thief has long been sought at the Memorial Library and Helen C. White Library at UW-Madison, where students spend hours studying and sleeping, often kicking off their shoes beneath the tables or in carrels or study rooms. During six weeks in the summer of 1988, for example, 12 pair of shoes valued at between $25 and $100 each, mostly slip-ons, were stolen from the two libraries. Typically, a student would take a pause in studies to get a drink of water, then return to discover shoes missing.

Police stepped up foot patrols in the libraries with no success.

The break in this case came shortly after a pair of shoes was stolen from a student at Helen C. White on Dec. 9, Hanson said. The student victim and a friend saw a man standing around at the library "who did not look like he belonged there," and who had an extra pair of shoes sticking out of his backpack. The shoes were not the student's, but the man identified himself to the victim with an Iowa drivers license. When two more thefts were reported on the same day. Hanson got the identification from the student and called Dubuque police.

"It sounded a little odd asking, but I told them not to hang up, I was looking for a shoe-theft suspect," said Hanson.

Hanson said an identification was made and the man interviewed. The suspect is under the care of a therapist, Hanson said, and had been arrested last July at Milner Library at Illinois State for shoe theft.

He said the suspect described making regular trips to Madison from Dubuque, parking at the Lake Street ramp, wandering over to one of the two large campus libraries and waiting for a chance to steal shoes. The suspect only rarely stole lace shoes, mostly men's shoes, and never athletic shoes.

There are at least 34 unsolved shoe theft cases pending, Hanson said.

The man had 80 pairs of shoes in his apartment, 60 of which he said he had purchased, Hanson said.

He told Hanson if the shoes fit, he kept them. Others he donated to charities. He said he only took shoes from campuses in Illinois and Wisconsin, none from Iowa.

■ **December 20, 1989**

Text, Lies and Videotape

The first few weeks of college life are difficult enough without having to acquire consumer detective skills to boot.

To help speed the process along, I will provide my own versions of several falsehoods a typical student is likely to encounter during these first days. The following statements, though often repeated, are seldom true:

■ We will return your security deposit at the end of the spring semester.

The Truth: We might return 25 percent of your security deposit, after you graduate, if you will re-roof our office building.

■ It takes three days for the spray to have an effect, then your apartment will be roach-free.

The Truth: If your apartment has roaches now, it will take until Valentine's Day to get rid of them.

■ This is the latest edition of this textbook, which will surely be used again next semester.

The Truth: This is the old edition, we already have the new edition in stock but we are dumping this edition on you so we don't have to buy it back at the end of the semester.

■ If more than enough students sign up, we will open up a new section.

The Truth: If more than enough students sign up, we will use the list of names to convince the administration we need more faculty, higher salaries, extra home computers and videotape cameras. We will sponsor a department picnic and Christmas party, which we will videotape. We might buy a department Isuzu Trooper to help our graduate students move to new apartments. We will certainly consider opening a new section the year after you graduate.

■ We can install your telephone between 8 a.m. and noon the day after tomorrow.

The Truth: We will arrive at your apartment 10 minutes after 1 p.m., five minutes after you have given up and gone back to campus to try to get into the closed section that was open this morning while you waited for us to arrive. Don't forget the security deposit.

■ The bus stops here every 20 minutes.

The Truth: Somewhere else the bus stops every 20 minutes. Not here, though. Not ever. No transfers, either.

■ This cheeseburger is only two minutes old.

The Truth: This cheeseburger has been under this heat lamp so long we have changed the ketchup twice and the onions have taken root in our special sauce, but you won't know it until you unwrap it and take a bite. Have a nice day.

■ Office hours are from 3 to 5 p.m. Tuesdays and Thursdays.

The Truth: Office hours are from 3 to 5 p.m. Tuesdays and Thursdays, but no one will be here.

■ If you aren't completely satisfied with your courses, instructors or textbooks, your money will be cheerfully refunded.

The Truth: You can keep your membership in the UW Credit Union.

■ Tennis court use for students and faculty only.

The Truth: Tennis court use for students and faculty only after legislators and spouses of staff are finished.

■ Your student loan will cover your first semester expenses for tuition, room and board.

The Truth: You will have to come up with living expenses yourself.

■ You don't need to buy a computer to be a successful student at UW-Madison.

The Truth: If you don't buy a computer from us, we will not allow you to register, eat in the dorm cafeteria, get dates, buy a touchtone telephone, work as a high-paid consultant for a computer company, order airline tickets, or get on our alumni mailing list. You will never own a car with power locks and you won't be allowed to buy anything with a Bucky Badger on it. We will haunt you for the rest of your productive life and tell your neighbors you don't have a computer. Your children, in short, will have no one to play with. You can join the UW Credit Union, though. ■ **August 30, 1988**

Customers Get Wrapped Up in Deception

There is a point where expectation overshadows reality, and there has never been a shortage of entrepreneurs willing to cash in on that.

If, for example, I charged you $35 for the chance to be wrapped in cloth soaked with manhole cover sealant, would you pay it?

How about if I said that by getting that wrap, you would "lose 20 inches"?

This is an example of how trying to alter an appearance can be deceiving.

And how a business man blew into Madison last summer, fleeced the locals, and slipped out just as the weather got cold and the local authorities got hot on his trail.

He was Robert W. Johnson, described by one Justice Department investigator as a "pinky-ring kind of guy."

Johnson opened Bodywrap USA in the second week of August at 658 S. Gammon Road. He promised his customers would lose inches. Bodywrap USA would remove toxins and firm up the flab, he guaranteed.

(This process is not new, even to Madison. In 1981 a similar bodywrap salon opened, offering a wrap in "dead sea salts" and another salon wrapped women in body cream and plastic wrap.)

The evidence is that Johnson didn't pay his rent, he didn't pay his employees, he didn't even pay for some of his radio and newspaper advertising.

And his customers?

For $35 or more per session, they were treated to a complete wrapping of their naked bodies in elastic bandages that had been soaked in a special "sea clay" and warmed in a Nesco roaster. Before a customer was encased, the body was measured in 26 places. After an hour in the mudwrap, the bandages were removed and the body remeasured.

Here's how one customer—who filed a complaint with the Justice Department after Bodywrap's closing was publicized—described what happened next:

"After finishing the session, the girl who wrapped me was all excited that I had lost 19 inches. But looking in the mirror, I really couldn't tell too much. Then she takes you to a room to talk with Robert Johnson who acts all excited about how much you've lost—he goes on and on. He doesn't give you much of a chance to talk, he's very intimidating. I signed up for three more sessions. . . . I don't know why, but with all those people telling you how great you look and you've lost so many inches, it was hard not to sign up for more and he was very insistent on paying in advance."

Some did. A Mount Horeb woman wrote out a $396 check for eight future wraps.

Johnson cut corners as well as inches.

For example, when he started he was using "Dr. Strem's patented formula" sea clay from Florida.

After Johnson left town, investigators found in his rented duplex garage evidence that in the last weeks of his business he had been mixing his own "sea clay."

This stuff was a type of powder purchased in 50-pound bags from a local supply company. The common use for Johnson's substitute "sea clay," investigators were told, is as a sealant around manhole covers.

So, Johnson wrapped his customers in elastic bandages soaked in a manhole cover sealant, heated in a chicken roaster. Customers who complained—and only seven have done so—to the Justice Department believe the measurements made on their bodies were rigged. If you measure the body in 26 places, it doesn't take much to claim a six-inch "reduction" after standing encased in clay for an hour.

Wrote one man who was told he had "lost" 19 inches: "I guess I deserve to lose the $35 because I was dumb enough to fall for this in the first place. However, I hope you nail the sleazeball."

"Nailing the sleazeball" may prove difficult.

Johnson and his family left town over the weekend of Dec. 10.

Steve Nicks, an assistant attorney general, said he believes Johnson sold a lot of package-deals to customers who are embarrassed to complain about it.

"We're still looking for people who may have bought those package deals," Nicks said.

Nicks has a good idea why Johnson left.

Since Bodywrap opened last August, the Justice Department was trying to get Johnson to provide proof for his advertising claims. In the end, the Food and Drug Administration on Nov. 25 provided an analysis of those claims, writing bluntly that the claims were "false and misleading or otherwise contrary to fact."

And, for good measure, the FDA called the bodywrap a "gross deception."

The Justice Department sent this letter to Johnson, and Johnson responded by absconding, with inches to spare.

Still, did Johnson deliver what he promised?

Inches were lost, and brochures clearly explain to customers there will be no weight loss.

Did Johnson leave town as a successful swindler? Or as a failed businessman? Were his customers victims? Or were they people who had unrealistic expectations?

William Lewis, a Madison attorney who helped Johnson incorporate his business and who represented Johnson in early discussions with the Justice Department, said he doubts that Johnson "made off with a stack of cash. He was having trouble making a living here."

Lewis said he was not aware of and did not condone any illegal business practices or unpaid debts by Johnson.

He said the nature of the business Johnson was in would eventually lead to customer disappointment.

"The vanity business is an area fraught with people (customers) who get all fired up about a new thing, hoping to find a new 'them,' then get all disappointed when there are no large changes," Lewis said.

"Nothing like that will ever change the inner you," he said.

He said Johnson, a Milwaukee native, was simply selling a "skin tightener."

"It was a poor person's tummy-tuck or face-lift," Lewis said.

The standard Bodywrap USA Instant Inch Loss Center newspaper advertisement promised the customer would "lose 6-20 inches in less than 2 hours, guaranteed or you pay nothing."

It featured a mini-bikini-clad young woman, pictured bending over, measuring her leg.

The ad said the bodywrap techniques "compact fatty tissue and actually smooth out bulges and unsightly cellulite."

And the promotional introduction guarantees that "all inches taken off on the introductory wrap will stay off."

And if they don't?

The guarantee provides for another body wrap, absolutely free.

And that is exactly what it was worth in the first place.

■ **December 19, 1989**

If You Were Swindled, Check It Out

Ed Negrin is a guy serving 14 years in a state prison in Arizona on a fraud conviction and he wants to be your friend, to give you money.

He called the other day from a pay phone at Fort Grant, Ariz.

If you owned a hotel or motel or resort or restaurant in Wisconsin between 1979 and 1984, you might remember him not so fondly by the names of "James Derman" or "Seth Thomas."

Under those names, he says, he bounced about $1.2 million in bad checks across the Midwest, including Wisconsin, one of his favorite states. He had gone to Arizona with a $111,000 grubstake—thanks to his victims in the Midwest—to start another life.

It shouldn't be necessary to point out that Negrin called because he is writing a book. Even a federal prisoner knows how to pitch a book.

And he called because he wants everyone he stiffed in Wisconsin to get on a list to get their money back.

Madison police have no record of any bounced checks under any of his names from those years, but he claims he was here and he wrote a lot of checks.

"I liked Wisconsin," said Negrin.

"The people are friendly and they don't ask a lot of questions, especially about checks written on out-of-state banks," he said.

"I never went to Milwaukee, it's too big of a city to do the kinds of things I was doing," he said.

Instead, he went to Markesan, Dalton, Madison, Rhinelander, Ripon and Green Lake.

"A lot of my checks were drawn on a bank that was closed, and they would give me cash," he said.

"The book is not on the shelves, it may be by the end of this year. It's not an autobiography, but it's about fraud protection for people and businesses," he said.

"I'll profile a confidence man, have a chapter about how to avoid being a victim," he said.

"I contend that I am completely responsible for my actions, but you might call some of my victims accomplices," he said. "That's why I'm including a chapter on checking out references, phony charities, bogus businesses."

Negrin did not go to jail because of checks bounced ("hanging paper," some call it) in Wisconsin or other Midwestern states. (He is from Illinois.)

He went because of a fraud charge connected with deceptive fund raising for a charity for missing children in Arizona, which he had been promoting, using the name James Derman, from the office of an Arizona senator.

His attorney, Robert L. Stewart, said the restitution offer is on the up-and-up. Negrin owes about $22,000 to 14 businesses who signed on when he was convicted, Stewart said. Royalties from his book will pay off that, and anything left will go to pay off people who sign on as victims, including those from Wisconsin. Stewart said his Phoenix law firm is not paid on a percentage basis, and he set up the restitution program at the request of a client who works with a prison inmate program.

Stewart said a few people have written claiming to be victims.

Negrin wants these people to tell him how he happened to swindle them. When his book sells, he will pay people back.

Negrin is a smooth talker and a bright fellow. He has been promoting this unwritten book for more than a year now, getting favorable publicity in radio interviews in Arizona and articles in several newspapers in the Midwest and West. Not bad for a prison inmate who used a missing-children front to steal money. And yes, he does have a book contract now, which accounts for this latest round of publicity.

No one has pointed out yet that the list of victims might show up in his book. People Negrin swindled will be writing him to describe his actions. He told me his book is not finished. And while he didn't say so, this sounds to me like a painless way to get background information to pad out his book. Negrin told me he doesn't have a list of victims or places. This would provide it not only for restitution—again, if his book sells—but for book information.

If I were one of his victims, I'd certainly put in to get the money back. I'd also suggest the incident be excluded from the book. After all, I wouldn't want to be another one of his greedy accomplices.   ■ May 7, 1989

Salesman Cleans Up, And Eats Up

ust another day in the suburbs.

A 71-year-old woman got a telephone call at her McFarland home offering a free carpet shampoo. It shouldn't take more than a couple of hours, given by a fellow who will try to sell a vacuum cleaner.

Certainly, says the woman. The carpet could use the cleaning and I could use the company.

A date in late April is set. The time is 2 p.m.

The fellow shows up and, while cleaning the carpet, tries to sell the woman a Kirby vacuum cleaner.

"The entire time he was there, and he was there until after 6 p.m., he tried to sell my mother a vacuum cleaner," claimed Janice Mashak, who this week filed a consumer complaint with the Justice Department's Office of Consumer Protection and Citizens Advocacy. The company is Midwest Kirby Vacuum Cleaners.

"She kept saying she couldn't afford it," said Mashak, noting the vacuum cleaner was a $1,100 model and her mother had a perfectly working Electrolux.

"And then he started drawing up the sales papers," she said.

"He asked her if she had anything she could trade for the vacuum cleaner," said Mashak.

He pointed at a lamp, could she trade that? She said no.

The woman had received a metal detector as a gift. It was in the closet. The salesman asked her if she could trade that. She said no.

Anything else of value she might trade?

How about the lawnmower?

The woman had a brand-new self-propelled lawnmower.

In the end, she traded the lawnmower, her Electrolux and $540 for a new Kirby vacuum cleaner.

During the trade conversation, the salesman told the old woman that others have traded for a vacuum cleaner. That was how he got his car, he said.

Mashak said that by the time the deal was closed, it was 6 p.m.

"He told her he had been working so hard all day that he was hungry, and then he conned her into making him supper," said Mashak.

It was not until a week later that Mashak heard about the deal from her mother.

"She lives alone on Social Security. She was perfectly happy with her old vacuum cleaner. She was just so embarrassed she didn't want to say anything about it," said Mashak.

Mashak called the Kirby people and tried to stop the sale.

"They told me the three-day wait was over, tough luck," she said.

Len Fox is the owner of Midwest Kirby. He tells a different story.

"If the woman would not have wanted the salesman there, the salesman would have left," said Fox.

"We see this once in a while, where the parents are perfectly happy with what they've done but the children want to save that money. They are overprotective and greedy. The woman probably wanted a Kirby vacuum cleaner all her life," said Fox.

Fox added that it is not unusual for Kirby salesmen to take items in trade for vacuum cleaners.

"We have a contest for the most unusual trade," he said.

"Beef, pork, motorcycles. I took a 44-passenger bus once in trade," Fox said.

As for his salesman talking himself into a free meal, Fox said, "he wouldn't have stayed if he wasn't invited. Some of these old people, you, know, you just can't get away from them."

So I called the woman:

"I was too ashamed to mention it to the kids," she said.

"He took my brand-new lawnmower and my vacuum cleaner that I bought only five or six years ago," she said.

"He said he was saving me all this money, now I have to go out and buy a lawnmower." she said.

Did he invite himself to dinner?

"Well, he said he hadn't had anything to eat since 10 a.m., and it was about 5 p.m., and he was giving me such a sad story I felt sorry for him. I said I got a casserole here and I'll warm it up, so we had casserole and some ham and strawberries and ice cream," she said.

"I really felt bad afterward, I was afraid to tell my one son," she said.

"I'll tell you one thing, from now on there's no salesman coming through this door," she said.

She called the salesman and asked for her lawnmower back.

"He told me I could have it back. For $300." ■ **May 21, 1989**

If Only We had the Secret to the Lottery

S o, you haven't won the lottery yet? You've spent mega-bucks and gotten mega-zilch in return? You buy a ticket and "sign immediately" on the line, imagining that you will really need to know that "by law, this ticket is the only valid receipt for winning a prize?"

I know why we lost.

It's because we didn't have "Al Capone's Lottery Busting Secret," as offered for a paltry $9.95 from Vegas Publications, of 1350 East Flamingo, Suite 28, Las Vegas, Nev., 89119.

That's right. It's time for another edition of How Dumb Do They Think We Are, in which we reveal the obvious flims, knee-slapping flams and various mail-order techniques designed to separate the rubes from their rubles and the gold from the gullible.

And at the top of a very high HDDTTWA stack is "Al Capone's Lottery Busting Secret," which has poetic justice written all over it, namely because, when you think of it, who better than a crook to advise anyone about the lottery.

The come-on is a "Dear Friend" letter from Tony Lobianco, a "trusted friend." Lobianco promises to "reveal a closely guarded secret so powerful it can change your life forever." And so "closely guarded" that it is being offered to only a select few hundred thousand or so.

Lobianco's story is this: Capone ran a "legitimate" illegal numbers game in Chicago and played the lottery himself, daily. To "protect his financial empire," Capone hired the best-known experts available to find out how the game could be beaten. Lobianco got the secret from a friend named "Joe," who one day in the early 1930s, while working as a numbers runner, delivered a package to Capone and overheard "the secret."

Capone, discovering "Joe," "walked across the room, looked into his eyes and said 'Kid, if you ever repeat what you heard, you'll never hear anything again.'"

Unfortunately for Joe, he kept his secret until three years‾ ago when, at 71, he was just about to use the secret when he got sick and was rushed to the hospital. This is where Lobianco the "trusted friend" comes in. Joe told Lobianco the secret, but only if Lobianco "promised to make this lottery-busting system available to anyone who needed money and would benefit from getting rich."

That narrows it down.

So he is selling the secret, right?

Wrong (no wonder you haven't won the lottery yet).

For $9.95, he will use the secret to figure out "your own private and confidential winning numbers."

"Use your private lottery numbers for 90 days. Then write and tell me how many lotteries you have won . . . tell me how much money you have earned . . . and, I will send you Al Capone's secret absolutely free."

Get it?

The secret is free. The numbers cost $9.95.

Personally, Lobianco adds, "I really don't want a whole lot of people to know about this."

I can see why.

■　　■　　■

Have you ever wondered how a journalist could afford to drive around in a 10-year-old car, eat at the swankiest of department stores and travel to most exotic of Wisconsin River sand bars?

Well, perhaps you have not received your bulk-rate offer from the Pase Literary Society, which guarantees an "ironclad" $1,000 writing assignment.

All this as a reward for joining the Pase Literary Society, of Aurora, Ill.

And, the PLS is "so sure you will be delighted with your new career as a writer that we will waive the usual restrictions and allow you to give it a try for three months."

I could not find any usual, or even unusual, restrictions, save for the $49-membership fee.

But what's $49 if I am to get a $1,000 writing assignment, guaranteed.

The assignment, according to the professional writers at Pase, "will attempt to be compatible with your interests and tendencies in an effort to make it easier for you to complete and get paid your $1,000."

Pase tells the wary HDDTTWA staff that the literary society is the "product development arm" of Pase Publications, a "multi-million dollar publishing firm." Pase knows that potential professional writers, of which I are one, "don't want to mess around with the nonsense of selling or rejection, and you want to earn money writing."

I was reading through the Pase brochure, suffering silently at the grammar errors, until I got to this sentence:

"It is a mutually beneficial arrangement that can work for both of us."

Everyone knows that a professional writer would have written:

"It is a mutually beneficial arrangement that can work for both of us together."

And that is a death bed confession that Lobianco would have been proud of. ■ **September 17, 1989**

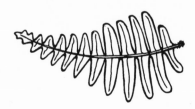

Stevens Point Could Relate to Randolph

The day the flimflam man came to town, he was escorted by a state development official. He was called "doctor," and he promised the moon and the stars and, in exchange, he suggested the city buy 40 acres for his factory.

Something did not sit right, though.

So the city's boosters talked to their bankers, and their bankers called bankers in New York. . . .

This is not a story about Randolph, the village that background-checking forgot. That community recently had its pockets picked by a fellow from New York who promised a remodeled factory and jobs in return for a $250,000 loan. Actually, he considered the money a gift, and that is a contentious subject right now in Jung country. No factory, no jobs, no money back.

And there, but for the grace of a suspicious banker or two, went Stevens Point, in 1957.

Philip Sundal was a rookie in the state's new industrial development office, under the auspices of the governor.

"We were contacted by a 'Dr. Mackenzie' of the New York area. A White Plains address gave him a touch of class. He wanted to set up a meeting with our major potato growers. He wanted to construct a plant to process potatoes, making things like frozen fries," Sundal remembered.

"He was quite well-informed about the state's potato crop and had a good vocabulary for discussing processing technology," Sundal said.

"It seemed like a winner. Ore-Ida had just made a quick reconnaissance trip. University Extension had just put out a piece on the good potentials for adding value to the state's potato crop."

Sundal, a researcher-writer now retired, was given the job as escort when Mackenzie came to town. They drove to Stevens Point, the Central Sands area and potato hot spot of Wisconsin.

Sundal recalled there was a "good turnout, from potato growers to bankers," to hear Mackenzie's pitch, but the locals "were real cool; they wanted more details."

"We started out for Madison, the 'doctor' was mighty quiet, and I was at a loss for words," Sundal said. "Just past DeForest, he began mumbling about the stupid jerks who couldn't see his great proposal. Suddenly he floored the big Caddy. We were racing down Highway 51 in the middle of the road. Cars everywhere were taking to the ditch. It was an awful trip, as I duly reported.

"The Stevens Point people made contacts in New York before we got our wits together to do the same. They found out that Dr. Mackenzie had a history of selling stock in companies that didn't exist. To our dismay, many communities heard about our ineptness in handling this 'prospect.'"

Roy Menzel, now retired from a public relations career, still lives in Stevens Point. He was chairman of the Stevens Point industrial development corporation when Sundal brought the doctor to town.

"He called himself doctor, and I'm not quite sure whether he was one or not, but he loved being called that. He did this in a number of communities in different states, and he loved the dinners and the attention," Menzel said.

"What I remember was when he left, he asked us to buy 40 acres on the corner of Highway J and Highway 10, which stretched back to the Soo Line railroad tracks. Then, while we were all enthused and excited, he said we better buy another 80 acres across the highway for residential development," Menzel remembered.

"That may have set us thinking that it sounded too good, so we started to make a few calls, and we had our banker friends make a few calls.

"At first it sounded as if he might be legitimate, and we felt embarrassed for even checking up on him. Finally, one of the bankers told our bankers that we had better be cautious, since there wasn't much of a bank account around his home," Menzel said.

Mackenzie was later arrested and charged in New York for selling stock in paper corporations, Sundal said.

But crook or not, Mackenzie may have been ahead of his time, Menzel said.

"It's kind of spooky, really, thinking about it now," he said.

"He was talking about freezing vegetables for shipment out on the rails. He had a heck of a good idea," Menzel said. "We ended up being the vegetable center of the state, with Del Monte, American Potato, Ore-Ida and Thermicold up here."

"We never prosecuted, nor did we ever consider that," Menzel said.

"He wasn't doing anything except stretching the ordinary fairy tale of everyday living a little bit," he said.

And, as Randolph just found out, fairy tales make thin soup.

■ **April 22, 1990**

A Glossary in Dealing for a Home

I took for gospel a real estate description of a house for sale.

Once.

You know the term, "stained glass windows?" Well, they were glass, and they were certainly stained.

Ba-dum. Hey, lighten up, you real estate agents, of whom there are 25,125 licensed brokers and 9,353 sales persons in Wisconsin (who generated only 434 consumer complaints to the Department of Regulation and Licensing in 1989). This isn't about real estate at all.

This is about words, and about how real estate descriptions sometimes imitate life, but seldom reflect it.

For example: "Wooded" lot, as in "lots for sale, some wooded."

As an adjective, "wooded" means "covered with wood."

In real estate descriptions, wooded really means covered with trees, and that can mean anywhere from three to 30 trees, probably closer to three because, if it were more than 30, it would say "heavily wooded."

What you will never read is: Lot with many (some, few, no) trees. "Wooded" sounds nicer, as does "gifted," which may mean covered with gifts or may mean having a gift, though few are said to "have a wood."

Next up: "Georgian," as in "smart Georgian-style home."

"Georgian" means of the artistic style of the periods of the reigns of George I, II, III and IV of England, 1714-1830. I am never clear whether that means the style of homes in Wisconsin during the reign of the Georges, which would be sod huts, caves and drafty log homes, or the style of homes in England at the time.

The same goes for next four reigns: Tudor, Victorian, Colonial, Ninja and Ranch. These are all "styles" of homes and salad dressings. "Beautiful two-story Victorian, less than 1 year old. . . ."

Then there is "Raised Ranch," a style of home that always has a deck, but is never at sea.

And "Exposed Ranch," which should be what happens when one is raised.

Stranger still, if it's not Colonial, Tudor, Victorian or Ranch, it's "traditional."

New in real life means, well, new.

Newer must mean even more new, right?

Wrong. In real estate, "newer" means "not as new as new, but not old," as in "Nice Tudor, newer carpet, furnace."

(This could be worse. Thinking of buying a newer car?)

Answer quickly: What is the difference between "custom remodeled," and "remodeled?"

In "custom remodeled," someone was paid to do it.

In "remodeled," someone did it for free.

And now some remodeled houses are being called "renewed." (See above.)

"Within walking distance": If you park close enough, it's flat and it's not winter, spring or fall.

"Natural woodwork": Woodwork.

"Original natural woodwork": Add $5 per foot.

"Contemporary": No woodwork, fake windowpanes.

"Motivated Seller": Can't handle two mortgage payments per month.

"Conveniently located": Truck stop next door is open 24 hours.

"Elegant": Old.

"Elegant and charming": Old and small.

"Wife-saver kitchen": Real estate agent is male, over 40.

"Landscaped": Mowed.

"Fenced yard": Bare lawn from previous owner's dog.

"Executive home": Expensive home with automatic garage door opener.

"European kitchen": Pots and pans hanging from the ceiling.

"Rustic": Fake beams.

"Starter house": Unfinished.

"Bonus room": Too small to be a bedroom, too large for a closet.

"Why pay rent?": No garage, no yard, no dining room.

"Reasonable": Seven percent.

"Unreasonable": Four percent.

"Don't be fooled": Be fooled.

"Updated electrical": City inspected.

"Enhances": Disguises.

"Many perennials": Knew last fall the house would be for sale.

"Dramatic": High, or big.

"Move-in condition": Vacant for six months.

"Classic": See "Elegant."

"Shaded": Grocery store next door. Not wooded.

So, the final advertisement is:

FOR SALE: Tudor style custom elegant charming cozy raised ranch on heavily wooded lot that enhances reasonable commission. Eat-in kitchen, newer updated mechanicals. Fenced yard, move-in tomorrow. Why pay rent?

Translation: Vacant trailer home for sale. Stained glass windows. ■ **April 8, 1990**

The Real Story About Buying Real Estate

Now, as the man says, is the time to buy. I think he really meant steal.

When I had my first house for sale, a real estate salesman came to look at it for five minutes, said he had a couple interested in buying it, and all he could do was complain.

There were cracks in the ceilings.

The bedrooms were too small.

The basement steps were too narrow.

He did everything except charge us for forcing him to see our pitiful hovel. I was surprised that he didn't discard his clothing after the tour.

Fortunately, I had already read a couple shelves of books about house-selling, and I knew this guy was using one of the oldest profession's oldest tricks: He was sent to talk trash about my house so that I would lower the price, resulting in quicker, easier money for the listing real estate company.

(I didn't lower the price. I had already paid for an independent—that is, not done by a real estate company—appraisal of my home, so I knew I was in the ballpark.)

Welcome to the season of home buying, selling, financing and hyping. After buying two houses and selling one, I have learned that the trouble with home buying is that you make all these mistakes, then there is really no way to learn from them. After all, how many more houses do I really expect to buy?

So, with full knowledge that these are my own experiences, here are some things I have learned about buying and selling houses:

Don't believe any house descriptions you read, especially in those little pulp pamphlets that give you photographs of houses for sale, but don't give prices or addresses. That way, you have to call the real estate company and you can't drive by to make a quick decision.

If a house has been "owner-built," bring your tape measure when you look at it. Only a last-minute inspection by a plumber friend of mine kept me from buying a home that had staircases 8 inches narrower than usual. (I later read that most furniture and appliances are manufactured so that they can be moved up and down the width of a normal staircase. If I had bought this house, my sofa would still be in the driveway.)

The salesperson is not your friend. He or she is paid on commission. If you are treated unfairly, don't wait around, dump him or her and tell the real estate company owners why. Likewise, if a good job is done, pass along the praise.

No matter when your house is sold, or for sale, or taken off the market, the sign in your yard will not be put up or taken down on time. I took one down by myself once and threw it in the ditch. It's my yard, isn't it?

If a salesperson asks you to lie about something, dump him or her immediately. I remember one who told my wife to lie about her income so we could get financing faster.

Get it in writing. I bought a house that the owner promised would be cleaned. He also promised to fix a large hole in the wall. Nothing was in writing, the house was dirty and I fixed the hole myself.

If you buy a house, you will have a "closing," which is another word for "opening" as in "opening a can of worms."

My advice on closing: bring your own attorney and ask questions. If it seems like the "closer" doesn't know what he or she is talking about, ask. I did this at my last closing. Turns out this was the closer's first closing and she did not know what she was talking about. If everyone is in a hurry, demand the commission be reduced.

No matter how much you ask or investigate, you will never find anyone who has ever really needed title insurance, except for the people selling it. They need it because it is free money and there is no way in hell you are going to avoid paying it because there are people down there selling it, too.

In Wisconsin, houses on hills are for sale only in the summer for good reason.

If there is something in all of those papers you sign at the closing that you do not want to go along with, don't sign. Believe it or not, there are other banks or institutions willing to take on the hardship of loaning you a lot of money at an outrageous interest rate and with closing costs that have no relationship to reality.

In arranging a mortgage, watch out for the word "point."

A "point" is a lot of money that you have to pay a stranger to rob you. This is not to be confused with an "origination fee," which is a lot of money you have to pay to a stranger to take your money in return for doing nothing at all.

I'm a little fuzzy on the technicalities, but I figured mine this way:

Walk in the door and approach the bank's counter. That is worth one point, or 1 percent of the total amount of money you want to borrow. Using the bank's pencil will put you in the "origination fee" category, figure one-third of one point. Sit in a bank chair while talking to the loan officer, another third of a point. The higher the number of points, the more likely it is that you will never be able to afford another house. But who wants to move, anyway. ■ **April 16, 1989**

Waterfelons Cardinal Sin in Wisconsin

It was the second week of May, and Leo Zanoni, from his office in Kalamazoo, Mich., had a surprise planned for Madison.

Zanoni, a watermelon specialist for Upjohn's Asgrow Fresh seed company, had instigated a secret shipment of 800 watermelons from Texas and Mexico growers to a produce store in Madison.

This was no ordinary watermelon.

"It was adapted for growers in Texas and Mexico," Zanoni

said. And it was developed so it would be very sweet and slice easily because "there is a trend in stores for sliced melons." It also had a pink-red color and was called "Cardinal" watermelon.

The test-growing was limited, and Zanoni wanted to test market the product. A Milwaukee native, he decided Wisconsin in the springtime was perfect for an "out-of-season" watermelon taste test.

He set everything up through a Jefferson public relations firm, Morgan and Myer. The melons would be sold at Brennan's in Madison.

Customers at the store would be greeted by university students who would vary their pitches about the watermelon.

One pitch would be for the watermelon being nutritious, and the next pitch would be for the watermelon's unique taste. If a customer actually bought a watermelon, the customer would then be asked at the checkout why the watermelon was purchased.

A newspaper advertisement said: "Try Delicious Cardinal Watermelon. Nutritious, High: Vitamin A & C. Iron. Potassium. No Fat. Low Sodium."

It was at this point that Wisconsin's watermelon police at the Department of Agriculture, Trade and Consumer Protection made an unexpected entrance into Zanoni's taste test.

Food labeling experts saw the ad and, while it may be acceptable to say watermelon is nutritional, it is not OK to say this particular watermelon is more nutritional than any other watermelon.

It was not that those claims were false; it's just that they are true for all watermelons.

The state confiscated the watermelons, a Brennan's manager said.

"We did not confiscate them," Terry Burkhardt, of the agriculture department, objected.

"We detained them for a period, and then they were released," he said.

"They were claiming that this particular brand was superior to other types of watermelon, and that is misleading the consumer because all watermelons possess those particular qualities," Burkhardt said.

And, he said, if a product is going to carry claims of one type of nutrition or another, it is going to have to have a label.

Watermelon labeling?

Yes, but only if they go about making these claims. A basic consumer right is for advertising to be accurate, and for that accuracy to be proven.

Zanoni does not want to start a food fight over this.

"Hey, I'm an aggie, I just wanted to see how they liked the watermelon," he said. The nutritional information was for watermelon, period, not necessarily Cardinal watermelon.

"They said our [sign] implied that the brand name was one thing, and not watermelon in general. Hey, they impounded the watermelon and I thought 'geez.' My approach would have been, if they say there's a problem, all we had to do was redo the signs," he said.

But the watermelon police ordered up a Dane County Circuit Court charge of "causing a false and misleading advertisement," a charge that was settled last week when the public relations firm paid a $307 fine and admitted Cardinal watermelon is no more nutritious than any other watermelon.

"If you really want my analysis, it was a bunch of miscommunication. We ended up saying, 'to hell with it, pay the darn fine,'" said Zanoni, who last week just happened to be addressing the

Watermelon Growers Association at the national Food Marketing Association convention in Memphis, Tenn.

And the topic of the "Wisconsin experience" was brought up, Zanoni said, because "It's obvious retailers want to talk about nutrition but don't know what sources they can use."

So he got the association this week to spend $12,000 on tests to properly analyze a watermelon so retailers could be confident they could publish nutritional information."

Zanoni said he was not a professional marketer or advertising genius, but he has considered putting nutritional labels on watermelon.

Burkhardt was worried this would be a "derogatory" story.

I can see his point. After all, "detaining" watermelons leaves me with visions of a state-run watermelon refugee camp.

Somewhere, though, this bit of enforcement got out of control, leaving a sour taste. Eventually, even Zanoni agrees better nutritional labeling on produce will be the result.

And how were the watermelons?

They sold out. Even the detainees.   ■ **October 30, 1988**

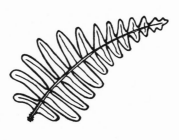

More
Real Life

The Romance of Woodburning

I have ceased taking a romantic pose about burning wood.

Greg Isaksen warned me about this, several years ago, when he sold wood stoves out of a pole shed in Poynette.

"If you're in it for the smell of the smoke and the exercise, I give you two years," he said.

I agree. I was thinking about the romance of woodburning the other evening. Darkness had already fallen over me like a stinky wet wool coat. I stood shivering next to my wood-hauling trailer in the back yard, breaking twigs off a dry old hickory branch. I broke off pieces about a foot long and placed them in the trailer. I had the trailer about half-full of kindling when I stopped and covered the pile with the boys' hard plastic swimming pool, tossing a couple of snags on top to keep it from blowing away.

One day next January I will burrow out to the trailer and find this precious supply of dry kindling. You can never have enough money, love or kindling.

Then there is the romantic problem of replacing ax handles.

I was at Farm and Fleet one afternoon last week, looking for an ax handle. Like most wood burners, I have an assortment of axes, mauls and hand-me-down wedges. I broke an ax handle last spring and am just getting around to buying a new one. If you shop at dear old Farm and Fleet, you are probably aware of its incomprehensible arrangement of goods. The ax department is a great example.

In one row at the front of the store are the axes, mauls and wedges. No ax handles.

The ax handles—but not the axes—are way over in the farm supply section. The little metal wedges needed to secure the ax to the handle are not with the handles, but in the ax department.

I bought an ax handle for about $5. I got the ax head and the handle together and they didn't fit, so I planed away a little all around and it still didn't fit. That was when I got the old broken handle out and measured it against the new handle and discovered I had bought a wrong-sized handle that was now in now condition to be returned.

I finally bought a handle that fit, at Sears, for $7.50.

This was all after I endured the romance of cleaning the chimneys. I cleaned them last spring, too, but in the fall I do it again just because I can never remember if I did it last spring. And I caulked around the flashing of the chimney. My ladder is three feet shorter this fall because I cut three feet off to get it up in the stairwell this summer when I was painting. I could use those three feet back, since now the ladder doesn't stick up above the roof when I need to climb up there to clean out the eaves troughs and caulk the chimney flashing.

So I have to put the ladder on the deck that didn't get painted this summer because I was out looking for firewood.

The stove needed cleaning and a little touch-up paint. The linoleum on the stair landing has a couple of deep nicks where the logs fell when the boys pushed them down the steps. Several hundred dollars' worth of Legos and Duplos in the house and my boys push logs down steps for entertainment.

I got most of my wood this year from a nice woman who had

a maple tree cut down by a fellow who not only left the wood from the maple, but also secretly unloaded onto her lawn the wood in his truck from another cutting job.

Anyway I have now logged 10 years of scrounging, cutting, splitting, stacking and burning wood, of sparks on the carpet, slivers in my gloves and burns on my wrists. And that means 10 years of ashes in the compost, warning tickets for unpredictable trailer lights, wrong-sized ax handles, head lumps from spring-back wood-splitting and backaches from a too-low sawbuck that I am too lazy to rebuild higher.

After 10 years of all that, a wood-stove fire is still my warmth of choice.

That and I like the exercise and the smell of wood smoke, of course. ■ **October 20, 1988**

Hubba-Hubba Doesn't Cap It

*O*ne day a long time I ago I answered an ad in the paper and went to look at a wood-hauling trailer for sale for $150.

As trailers go, it was ordinary. That is, the lights didn't work and there appeared to be a lot of spots where someone practiced welding pieces of iron together at unusual angles.

I bought the trailer.

I painted it. I re-wired it so the plug would fit the odd socket in my 1969 Volvo. I put new lenses on the lights. I put on a new tailgate and added a reflector or two. I replaced the front of it, too, with two-by-sixes.

After a Fitchburg cop stopped me at dusk one evening, I rewired again and fixed the safety chain.

Since I bought the trailer in 1978, I have hauled a lot of wood.

I hauled some willow abandoned near Picnic Point. It was easy to split but didn't heat. I hauled a baby crib and changing table from Wausau before the birth of Espen, who is now five.

I hauled a lot of oak out of rural Mount Vernon, and, as repayment, the trailer stayed in Mount Vernon to help a friend haul his wood. (Hence, new lenses again.)

I hauled a couple of loads of nice dry birch from a fuel oil place that used to give customers a load of wood free every winter.

I hauled five loads of stones a landscape specialist had deposited in a friend's side yard, before my friend bought the house and got another landscape specialist to say he didn't need all those rocks.

I hauled a load of sand for my son's first sandbox (since enlarged, as I now have two sons who cannot co-exist in a one-son-size sandbox).

I hauled several loads of household possessions from one house to another, fishtailing down Fish Hatchery Road.

I have backed that trailer into my driveway a hundred times and into tight spots between trees at night without jackknifing. Of course, that was always when I was alone.

During the day, and in front of snickering spectators, I have backed that trailer into a perfect V-shape several times.

I have filled that trailer with tons of kindling from a secret sawmill and with bushels of twigs from my own back yard.

I have crawled under that trailer just to see what it looks like under there.

I have moved a mountain of snow around that trailer while it was parked in the driveway over winter.

That trailer has never had a flat tire.

The day I bought it, I paid no attention to the hubcaps.

At the time, living near University Avenue, I had acquired a small collection of squashed hubcaps, collected on my walks. I replaced the two hubcaps on the trailer with a Buick cap and a Pontiac cap.

I can't recall what made me suspect those two old hubcaps were valuable, but one day it occurred to me that the emblem in the middle of the hubcap was not a crown, but an "E," and that the hubcaps were Edsel hubcaps.

So for several years now I have kept those hubcaps on a top shelf in the garage, earning unreported interest, I hoped.

What could these be worth? A trip to Europe? An evening meal with wine at the Ovens?

Into every life a cash-flow problem occasionally emerges, so last week I decided to put the family's Edsel hubcap collection (of two) on the market.

The ad cost me about $6 and I offered them for sale for "best offer." That way, I thought, I can accept the first three-figure offer that comes along. I'm not greedy.

I remembered the name of an Edsel collector and gave him a call.

How much, I asked, should I accept for these two hubcaps?

What kind of condition are they in?

One's got a couple of BB dents in it, I said, but otherwise they're in perfect shape.

Well, he said, there's a lot of Edsel hubcaps on the market.
(How could that be, I thought. They don't make these anymore.)

How much should I consider to be a best offer, I asked.

Well, he said, about $5 apiece.

Cancel my reservations. ■ **September 12, 1989**

Last Days of Hunting Season

*H*eard one too many deer-hunting stories?

Well, even if your blood doesn't run blaze orange, here's
another one.

A bologna sandwich and a paperback book are as important
to the late-season deer hunter as comfortable boots and warm
gloves.

You don't see any of those nostalgia pieces about deer hunting
in the paper after that first weekend.

That's because the last days of the deer-hunting season are
not filled with the camaraderie, poker and beer-and-dirty-joke
times of the first weekend.

I haven't pulled the trigger on a deer hunt since I was 19,
but when I remember those end-of-the-season deer-hunting
days, it is with the same fondness of the first time I fell off a
barn roof. My first reaction when I fell off the roof was: What

the heck was I doing up here in the first place?

That last Sunday morning of the season, just be wearing blaze orange you may as well be wearing a sign that says "Loser," or at least "Lousy Shot."

Those hunters who know the territory already have their deer, some have two, having done some scouting long in advance, knowing exactly when the prize buck will be picking his way along the trail.

Only pride, embarrassment or a bet will bring a deer hunter to the woods on the last day of the season. Being a terribly impatient hunter myself, I have never believed those guys who explain their failure by saying they are just waiting for the "big rack."

A lot of it is family pride. Brothers, fathers, uncles will all pitch in to help the guy who "hasn't got his deer yet." And that guy feels just terrible about it.

The embarrassment isn't temporary, either. Remember that a teen-ager going deer hunting may, like me, have spent several evenings studying photographs and reading the narration on how to properly clean a deer, step by step. Soap and water does not enter the picture until hours later, and then not for the dead deer but for the hunter.

My manual came with the hunting knife my father gave me for Christmas many years ago. My brother got the exact same gift. (To this day, we get the same gifts for Christmas.) I was fascinated by the various methods pictured of carrying or dragging a deer carcass back to the car. Most unlikely, it seemed to me, was the illustration of the hunter with the deer over his shoulders. How does he do that? More likely, as I have experienced, the guy simply hollers for some help dragging the deer out of the woods.

I did not memorize the various methods pictured of deer carcass disposal.

What I did was carry the book with me, folded and in a pocket, along with a ring bologna sandwich, a thermos of coffee and a good paperback book. I would have made progress in the woods if I hadn't had to carry a rifle or shotgun.

While my brothers and father and uncles earnestly set about seeking deer, I found a stump, sat down, ate my sandwich right away, drank my coffee, got bored reading the book, paged through the photographs of the deer-killer's manual and then considered what kind of impact a shot from my deer rifle would make on a squirrel.

That last morning was the worst.

Deerless, cold, sandwich gone and tired of answering the "getcherdeer?" and "see-enny?" questions, sitting in the woods, missing the Packers game, the only thing left was to wait for the rest of the hunters and go on a "drive."

A "drive" is when, all else failing, hunters tromp loudly through the woods yelling "wooo-wooo" and "eeyah-eeyah" to scare the wily whitetail into flight, preferably in the direction of the strategically placed best shots in the group.

I was never strategically placed to shoot anything. I was one of the guys walking through ear-flap-high briars yelling "wooo-wooo."

That—and the fact I was shot at by a road-hunter once—is really why I quit deer hunting. Call me unsophisticated, but I could not picture myself, the big game hunter coming home after a day in the woods stalking, answering a question from my son about what I did that day.

"I was in the woods, yelling 'wooo-wooo.'" If I am going to drink coffee, read a paperback and eat bologna sandwiches, the closest I want to come to blaze orange is when I throw another log into the woodstove.

Besides, my brothers and father, who feel sorry for me, always drop off a couple of venison steaks.

■ **November 29, 1987**

So, you got home Sunday morning and you smelled like a wet wig.

Well, so did I.

There were glass bits in my tennies, my breath could have opened the garage door and my right elbow was sore from leaning on the wall next to the Goodwill Store.

My notebook got wet, too, but there were a few things I saw on State Street Halloween night . . .

At 7:40 p.m. police ticketed an eight-foot Cuervo tequila bottle (cardboard type) for carrying a drink from a Cuervo tequila bottle (glass quart type) in front of the Walgreen's at State and Lake streets. (I know it was Walgreen's because four guys were standing in front of it, dressed as a "Walgreen's" sign.) The bottle said later that his ticket cost him $69.50.

"I don't mind, it's part of the game," the bottle said. (His stash was poured into the storm sewer.) The game was discrete drinking, which in a wig-to-wiggle crowd, was not so difficult.

The key was to stay in a crowd.

Not like the fellow who pulled out a green bottle of beer one block from the Square.

He was spotted by a cop, who not only wrote a ticket, but made him donate his six-back to the root system of the tree in front of Jack's Shoes.

Another costume that didn't make it onto the street was the 12-foot by 12-foot jail cell, constructed of two-by-fours and hauled in from a side street by six guys who were stopped because the structure and prisoners were slightly unstable.

If you ever wondered where cute raisins keep their identification cards, check their feet.

Four raisin(ettes) each took off one shoe before entering the beer garden. The shoes held their money and their identification cards.

You had to be able to read the signs to tell what some of the costumes were. The superhero would have been just another superhero without the logo of "Mighty Malt."

The five peas in a pod costume was clever, as was the guy with them carrying the sign: "Peas be with you."

Before the rains came to mousse the masses and blur the bee stripes, there was time enough to notice a bumper crop of inflatables this year, especially the inflatable sex-dolls. There were too many. And you would have thought we had seen the last of the Blues Brothers years ago.

Also, all those public service ads and safe-sex messages must be doing some good. Organizers could have had a condom section this year. At least these people would have stayed dry.

Two guys with long foam-rubber penises on their heads had a standard response to the shocked shouts of observers: "Ah, you recognize us?"

It was mostly a yawner until the dunderheads got a King of the Mountain going on the Library Mall fountain cover.

Flying wedges of drunken men sought to overtake the top of the fountain cover. This went on for more than an hour, with hulking inebriates dive-bombing, blind-siding and clip-tackling each other for control of the fountain. It was like an uncontrolled dogfight, only cold water did nothing to stop them. The falls were hard, on to concrete, and watching it was painful and embarrassing. It was also embarrassing because police did nothing to stop it, though obviously people were getting hurt.

Thank the heavens for the rain. The beer garden and no-street-drinking-allowed trucks worked up to a point, though the beer gardens were too small and there were no separate exits, making people leave angry.

And it would have been a lot more fun if all the hard guy drunks had turned into pumpkins at 11 p.m., after which State Street was clearly a dangerous place to be.

■　　■　　■

This did not happen on State Street: Early one morning last week police were sent to Denny's Restaurant on the East Side. An off-duty restaurant employee was eating breakfast. It was his birthday so there was also a small birthday cake on the counter in front of him.

A woman who had already eaten came over and wanted some of the cake.

According to Officer Leonard Preston's report, the man "refused to give this woman the cake and she mentioned that if it was a certain flavor, mainly chocolate, that she would smear it all over her body and would let him lick it off. At that point, she lifted up her T-shirt and exposed her bare breasts. She was then told to leave."

The woman had long blond hair and was wearing sunglasses (this was at 2:15 a.m.) and a T-shirt with the words "Bar Bitch" written across the front of it.

She did as she was told. She left.

And, perhaps not coincidentally, she didn't pay for her breakfast.   ■ **November 3, 1987**

Never Prepared for Wisconsin Winter

The cold arrives like a car door on a finger. You don't know until the last moment it is coming, it hurts a little at first, then you vow not to be taken by surprise again.

Then it turns warm a while and you forget about it until it happens again.

In the meantime, all those fall chores have gone wanting. There are still leaves in the eaves, the anti-freeze is good only to 10-above and the package of tulip bulbs bought on sale is unopened on the garage workbench.

The lawn chairs have become cold-welded to the deck, the closet holds four right-hand gloves and only two left-hand gloves and there is fungus all over the leather winter boots.

This is a time for preventive maintenance for home and health in Wisconsin. The cupboard holds a family-size bottle of Vitamin C tablets. Families organize tissue coupon searches, then troop to the store and load up on nose-wipes. Everyone starts wearing slippers around the house.

On a recent evening more suited to watching *ALF* or playing Scrabble, I stood on a wobbly chair, hair-dryer in hand, trying to shrink a sheet of plastic around the bedroom window. The finished product looks like heck, the kids have learned a couple of new words, the hair dryer overheats and breaks the circuit and there is sticky-on-both-sides tape all over the bedspread. Also, I finally locate the missing scissors on the windowsill, between the plastic and the window.

But I have once again reduced the chances of coughing and sniffling my way through another Wisconsin winter.

■ **November 24, 1987**

Winter's Double Whammy

Puddles freeze in mid-ripple. Radial tires grow corners. It is too cold in the garage to fix new Christmas toys. Normally sane people wear argyle knee socks to bed.

It is the time to change gears. Real winter comes to Wisconsin. Time to bundle up and shut up, because talking wastes breath and puts salty icicles on the mustache.

Stick around here long enough and you will know that no calendar, weather map or computer graphic can predict when winter will arrive.

I say it showed up over the weekend, at about 6:15 p.m. Saturday, when it was not possible to walk to the neighbor's house 100 feet away without a hat on, without mittens. It was also when the neighbor's house was as far as I wanted to go on a Saturday night.

The real winter arrived in time to save a snowman in the back yard but not the bubble pipe, carrot and Groucho glasses-nose that had slipped earlier from his melting head. There it will now slump until March, a temporary landmark, a faceless, frozen lump with my Schmidt beer cap frozen fast to its linebacker neck.

Everything doubles when it turns cold. Instead of a pair of gloves, it is a pair of gloves and a pair of mittens pulled on over the gloves.

Instead of one pair of socks, it is two pair, replaced in shifts: start the week with two pair. The next day throw the inner pair in the laundry, put the outer pair on first and then a new outer pair, and so on.

Instead of 10 minutes to dress the kids, it is 20 minutes.

The irony of weather extremes is that on both sides—real cold and real hot—life slows down and practicality takes over. The result is by necessity more of a planned, orderly life. Even the hopelessly confused need to face a real winter with some sort of plan.

For many the plan is simple: Leave.

For others, coping with the real Wisconsin winter is no more complicated than putting on another sweater during the day, switching from cotton to flannel pajamas at night and muttering "dang fool" every time you see someone walking around outside without a hat.

Real winter also shortens outdoor conversations:

"Won't start eh?"

"Nope."

"Need a jump?"

"You got cables?"

"Yup."

"Give 'er a shot."

"There she goes."

"Later. Thanks."

And real winter lengthens indoor conversations:

"Time to go."

"What'sa thermometer say?"

"Ten below."

"Zero?"

"Zero."

"Any coffee left?"

"Still hot."

"I better have some."

"Help yourself."

"Any money left in the checkbook?"

"No."

"Oh."

"Need it?"

"No, just asking."

"Oh."

"Car running OK?"

"Little rattle when I idle."

"Me too."

"What?"

"I mean I rattle when I'm idle, too."

"What's that?"

"Never mind. It was a joke."

"What? Never mind? What joke?"

"Never mind."

"I better get going. Any more coffee?"

"A little."

"Why isn't there any money in the checkbook?"

"You need some?"

"Yeah, I guess."

"Why?"

"I thought I'd take the car to the shop. Got a rattle some-where."

"Kinda cold. Can it wait?"

"I guess. Mmmmbye."

"Mmmmbye. Stay warm."

"You too."   ■ **January 10, 1989**

Remember to Forget Some Things

 ome people make Christmas lists of things they have to remember. I suggest making one of things to forget.

Please forget to buy the beer and liquor for the family Christmas dinner. Or at least stop before you buy "plenty." It is my experience that it is better to run out of beer and liquor than it is to have more than enough. Excess drinking always leads to "you'll regret it" arguments at family holiday gatherings. Forget it.

Please forget to chide your relatives about their sudden change in religion, especially if the change was made because of "hypocrites in our other church."

And forget to ask how things went at the pro-Ollie rally.

And please, please don't mention diets, unless you are overweight.

That is allowed. The correct way to greet all relatives at a holiday gathering is: "Gee, have you lost a couple of pounds?"

Politics is out, too, unless it is old politics. Really old, which means before Lincoln.

So, forget about saying to your sister: "Geez, you're getting fat, must be that right-wing new religion of yours. Here, have another tequila slush."

Cars are OK to talk about, unless you feel a need to talk about the cost of the new family car. Don't do it. The old guys will rib you about paying too much, and the young guys will say it would have been better to lease.

While on the subject of money, ignore it. Until after Christmas. There is plenty of time up until Christmas for a relative to tear up a gift check.

Do not return a gift to the giver with the comment: "You have more use for this than me."

Help with the dishes, but forget the impulse to say: "I don't mind cleaning up, I have to do it enough at home." The act of helping is a good thing. Your everyday helper may hear you whining, and, what's worse, may even take you at your word and leave all that homework for you, since you take credit for it anyway.

This may sound anti-Midwestern, but forget about saving the gift wrapping paper. You will save it, fold it, pack it away and never, ever see it again.

Forget about your brother-in-law's suggestion to bring along the Rob Lowe videotape. If you haven't seen it yet, it is boring and fuzzy and not worth the time. Forget it.

Forget the notion that your nephews will be happy with new scarves for Christmas.

Forget the notion that you will be happy with a new scarf for Christmas.

Forget about your wish for a basketball backboard and pole for Christmas, because all of your relatives think you are too old for that sort of thing.

Please forget the impulse to buy a Christmas card that plays music.

And remember to forget to put blinking lights on the Christmas tree instead of lights that do nothing but sit there, lighted. Those "running lights" are OK for X-rated theater marquees.

And that urge to put only one color of lights on the tree? Forget it. Get some lights of all colors, unless you create sculptures of your outdoor lights, then one color is fine.

Finally, forget about driving home at night.

This is Wisconsin. The countryside looks great in the winter daytime, with vapor-wisps from farmhouse chimneys pushing into the sky, cows standing in steaming bunches with icicles hanging from their lower lips, stunned looks on their faces.

The fence posts are wearing cute little snow-helmets, the Mormon Tabernacle Choir tape is on, and, if you get off the interstate once in a while, you won't have to tolerate Illinois drivers pulling snowmobile-laden trailers at 85 mph in a snowstorm, fishtailing over three lanes, cutting off honest tax-paying Wisconsin residents who . . . oh, forget it.

■ **December 21, 1989**

Truly a Gift Worth Giving

When the box came to the hospital, tiny Anna went through the shipment of hats one by one. She was looking for the "beanie-copter," a hat with a propeller on it.

There was none, and that started a search to grant a Christmas wish, a search that united a worried grandmother in Sheboygan, a National Cancer Institute telephone counselor in Madison and a caring toy store employee.

Anna, a four-year-old from River Falls, is spending her holidays in the St. Paul (Minn.) Children's Hospital. Three weeks ago she had a slight fever. Today she has Burkitt's lymphoma, a rare, two-in-a-million, devastating cancer. She is being treated with chemotherapy, which has caused her hair to fall out.

One set of relatives sent her a box of hats, not an unusual therapy for someone who is undergoing chemotherapy.

But the girl looked through the box and did not find the hat she really wanted, the one with a propeller.

What grandmother can hear of such a wish from such a child and not be compelled to move heaven and earth to grant it? But the grandmother, who lives in Sheboygan, could find no beanie-copter.

So she called an 800 number (1-800-4-CANCER) that puts people in touch with the Cancer Information Service at the UW Clinical Cancer Center in Madison. The person who answered Wednesday was counselor Marsha Jaeger, who generally deals with what she called "the emotional aspects of cancer."

Jaeger said it was the first time she had taken a request for a hat.

"I'll try," she said, and she did, calling every toy store in Madison until she reached a fellow named Chip Mitchell at the Puzzlebox on State Street.

The store was sold out of beanie-copters, but he would find one, he told Jaeger. And he did, that afternoon, at the Puzzlebox in Milwaukee's Grand Avenue Mall.

Jaeger called Chip back, Chip said he found a hat, Jaeger called the grandmother in Sheboygan, who called the toy store in Milwaukee, which arranged for a multi-colored beanie-copter to be sent to Anna at St. Paul's Hospital, in time for Christmas.

The grandmother, who asked that her granddaughter's real name be kept secret, said the four-year-old is "a very determined little girl, a fighter.

"She didn't want a bonnet, she didn't want a wig, she wanted a beanie-copter. It seemed like a small request, but it was important to her, so it was important to me."

And others.   ■ December 23, 1989

Compassion Can be the Key to a New Year

The best thing about a new year is that you don't have to be rich to get one.

I am going to steal this idea for a column from Olav, the King of Norway.

In 1974 I was broke and alone on New Year's Eve, in the seventh month of what would eventually become more than two years of self-imposed exile in Norway.

For the holidays, my only luxuries were the bottles of beer I kept tied to a string and hung out a window to keep cold. So I was drinking cold beer and watching television on a set borrowed from a student down the hall who had gone home for the holidays.

Thinking of this, it doesn't really sound so bad. But late in the evening, I was just getting lonesome and miserable when the King came on with his New Year's message to the people of Norway.

The King of Norway is a hearty fellow who always looks like a pretty girl just unexpectedly kissed him on his cheek.

I don't remember most of what he said, but I do remember one thing.

After congratulating everyone on a great year and predicting a good year for everyone else, he looked right at me (I thought) and said something like this: "And especially to all you out there who are alone, or old, or sick, or poor, or down on your luck, I hope and pray that things get better."

That mushy message from the top guy warmed my tipsy heart that night and I can't remember it now without getting a little weepy.

The King's message—simplistic and inspirational, I know—is the message I was referring to earlier.

The new year is for everybody.

It's for the 30-year-old man who slept beneath a blanket behind a wind-stopping evergreen bush in Brittingham Park last night. May your new year find you a job.

It's for the old woman who has everything but company. May the new year give you a visitor bearing a loaf of bread, a pound of coffee and a jar of homemade blackberry jam.

It's for the cop who left for work early after a shouting match with his wife. May the new year give you a chance to sort it out.

It's for the disabled child who has two brothers and a teen-age mother. May the new year find you an angel.

It's for the retired bachelor with a bad knee who lives alone on his 40-acre beef farm. May the new year send you a euchre partner who values your friendship enough to lose a game once in a while.

It's for the immigrant who appears to have it all. May the new year find you a friend who understands that you can't leave loneliness.

It's for the family of five that rolled into town on the strength of a hope and a telephone number. May the new year allow you to develop, grow and prosper here. May the new year give you a chance to succeed without bitterness about where you have been. May it provide help with compassion, encouragement without pity.

And the new year is for you. If you are alone, or sick, or poor, or unhappy.

May your kindnesses in the new year be returned one-hundredfold.

May someone tell you that a small part of the world is a better place this year, because you are in it. ■ **January 1, 1989**

A Good Snowstorm Puts the Clichés Back into Winter

*I*t's about time. We got a real howler Tuesday and it's about time.

We've had such mild winters lately that my three-year-old son was starting to speak with a drawl.

Finally, we got a school-closing, trash-covering, mustache-frosting snowstorm and now are you happy?

After two winters of predicting a snowstorm, without any showing up, we got one. And, as my older brother would say, it was a doozy.

Writing this, I can look out the patio door window and wonder how deep the snow would be if it actually fell on the ground. It is falling horizontally. I think the snow is deeper on the side of the walnut trees than it is on the ground.

The snow has done some serious exterior decorating around the homestead. The ugly tarps that cover the woodpiles show through only in a few blue wrinkles. The muddy gashes created by recent power company work along these suburban Oregon-Fitchburg roads have disappeared beneath a white blanket.

The guys on the radio keep talking about the "road situation." It is a mark of a snowstorm that the media keep telling us the obvious. There's a blizzard going on and the radio guys are telling us the roads are bad. Still, listening to the radio on a snowstorm morning is as natural as stomping your feet before walking through the open front door. What school would remain open on such a day as Tuesday?

Madison School Superintendent James Travis waited until 6:30 a.m. on the button to say the Madison schools would not open. And he sounded so sad about it, even when one radio newsman fed him a great straight line.

After Travis said the schools would not open, the newsman asked him: "And why is that?"

What a good snowstorm does is put the clichés back into winter. It isn't snow, it's "white stuff." There is not an accumulation, there is a "total accumulation." Not only can we not see anything, there is "poor visibility."

The massive effort—I'll bet those snowplow drivers were wondering when they would ever get another chance at overtime—that goes into clearing snow from streets is measured in "pieces of equipment."

I plan to clear my driveway with four "pieces of equipment," three of them shovels, one of them so heavy it is useful on fog only.

The fourth "piece" is a tool I have desired for many years and finally bought a couple of months ago when Sutherland Lumber went out of business.

It is an aluminum "snow rake," used to pull snow from a roof. In previous winters, I have used a 15-foot two-by-two to which I had nailed a 3-foot piece of plywood. To get the darn thing on to the roof, I had to take a running-sliding start and slice with a whummph into the roof snowpile. What usually happened was the plywood got stuck on the first try and I would be left bouncing up and down on my end of the two-by-two, which remained imbedded in the roof until Easter.

With the new snow rake, I just may shovel the roof before I shovel the driveway.

First, though, I have to take care of a chore that I assume many other snowbounders will have to take care of before this snowstorm dwindles.

I have to sample the fresh Christmas cookies.

Five hours later my wife and I were at the front of the drive-way, waiting for Godot in the form of the snowplow. I refuse to shovel until the plow goes through and because I have to use the fog shovel. She claims that to shovel right away makes the shoveling easier after the plow goes through.

She is in charge of the cookies, so we shovel.

The plow goes through. That blanket of snow, so pretty from the vantage point of the living room window, is too darn heavy to admire anymore.　　　　　　　　　　　■ **December 16, 1987**

This Weather Doesn't Make Sense

*B*ecause they are longer, people don't wash them as often.

Long underwear, that is, and if that doesn't make any sense, not much does in this kind of weather.

Plastic doesn't make sense in this kind of weather. It breaks. Especially if it is attached to a car. Car door handles break. The knob on the heater fan breaks. The plastic garbage can breaks.

Food doesn't make sense in this weather. A person eats food to replace calories consumed in, ideally, exercise. But this weather is too cold for outdoor exercise and, well, the wheel spokes on an exercise bicycle aren't supposed to attract spider webs, are they?

Conversation doesn't make sense in this weather, unless it is about: the cold, the heating bill, the car that doesn't start, the car that does start, the people who work outside.

Clothes don't make any sense in this weather. All the lumpy people, where do they all come from? They stand in the hallway placing layer upon layer upon layer of clothing over their long johns while the car warms up, then they get to the car, which by that time is too warm to sit in while wearing all those clothes. So the scarf gets untied and the down coat unzipped— but not all the way, since it is impossible to get the zipper started, or even see it, over the flannel shirt and Icelandic wool sweater—and the mittens come off, all to be replaced, outside, in the cold parking lot, when the car reaches its destination. Makes no sense.

Work makes no sense. Newspaper photographers get assignments that read: Go take a picture of the cold. Couldn't they just get their "pictures of the heat" from last summer and reverse the negative?

Not even the garage makes sense. After the temperature drops below a certain point, and it is way below freezing in the garage, what's the benefit? And the freezer is in the garage, too, working overtime to keep the food cold?

■ **December 23, 1989**

Amid Spray of Crumbs Spring Springs

It's curious how spring chores change.

In springs past, by now I might have been unlacing the shoestrings that held my baseball glove in the "perfect pocket" position all winter. (For an even better pocket, I would drop the tied-up glove into a pail of water then let the glove dry around the softball and baseball left in the pocket.) Instead, I am cleaning cat poop from the sandbox.

I might have been shooting baskets on someone's driveway.

Instead, last Saturday I was using a leaking spray bottle to squirt a mixture of detergent and water on hordes of box elder bugs that made my south-side outside wall appear to undulate in the sun.

At least this spring I don't have to haul the high chair to the back porch for a hosing and some deft chisel work. The youngest, Eivind, has graduated to a big chair with a booster seat. This doesn't lessen the spring cleaning effort. The April shower in this house is the deluge of falling Teddy Graham crumbs, rice grains and dried noodles that hibernated to the recesses beneath the booster seat during the winter months.

So far, among other spring duties, I have twice evicted Oscar, the squirrel with no tail, from the comforts of the cave between the top sill of a window and the eave of the house. Oscar clatters up the side of the house and the window frame to get there.

The good news is that the 1988 drought didn't hurt my lawn a bit. The back yard looks exactly like a large version of the splotch of bald in front of a playground soccer goal. This is just what the lawn looked like before the drought. Properly aerated by a workaholic all-season mole with a sense of direction honed on tulip roots and coffee grounds, the lawn should stay green for, oh, several days between April 1 and October 1.

It is too early to worry about the lawn.

Spring is a time to defog the attic, to bang a two-by-four on the picnic table's hollow pipe legs to scare away the wasps, to wonder if those cheap trees I bought at discount stores during the drought will actually get leaves.

It is a time to wonder if it is cruel to stop feeding the birds, reasoning that they should be able, like graduate students, to make it on their own in the summer.

It is also a time to make a fairly big macho deal out of changing the oil in the car to "summer weight" oil.

I keep charts on this sort of thing. I can't remember if 10-W-30 is for the summer and 10-W-40 is the winter oil, or vice versa. I refer back to what oil I put in the car crankcase last summer, but I always doubt whether it was correct then and whether I will just be repeating my mistake.

I have a "summer weight" and a "winter weight," too.

In the winter, I weigh myself with all my clothes, boots and coat on. Then, when spring arrives, I weigh myself naked. This is a fast and foolproof (as in fool-proven) way to lose eight pounds—and clear out the bathroom.

And, I should write this with a whisper, the spring auction weekends have started.

Standing in a muddy farmyard on a Sunday afternoon bidding on antique Tupperware may not seem like an exciting way to spend a spring day. But an auction, particularly a farm auction, reveals a lot about life and death that you won't pick up in the video arcades. You can bid on history, on a family's disintegration, on someone's idea of a gag gift ("This is my anniversary present?") I have a list of things I need around the house that I always look for at auctions. The trouble is, they usually sell them in threes. Who needs three rug swatters?

I am never bored at an auction. An auction gives me comparisons. Not just in prices of treasures I have bought at other auctions, but in what I think is important. I put a big price on some things that others would barely bid on.

At the risk of romanticizing the process, an auction is an affirmation that not all lives are the same. Maybe it's because at an auction, just about everything is one-of-a-kind.

I know, it seems like a long way from spring, but I've found that springs are not all the same, either. ■ **April 4, 1989**

More Rain?
Less Stress

t is (mostly) just your imagination about the rain, but. . .
Do those late-arriving leaves on the hickory trees today
seem like they are ready to burst out of the branches? Like the
moment before the explosion while squeezing a plastic, capped,
ketchup bottle?

Is it just some romantic notion that a rain, a soaking, culvert-
cleaning, mulch-inflating rain can lure the green out from beneath
the earth and into the open?

Can a row of radish seedlings be coquettish? Are they now,
after the rain, peeking up and flirting—yes flirting—with the
sun? Warm me now. I'll grow.

Is it too farfetched to believe that somehow, it was known
that just-planted buttercup bulbs could use a dousing, that the
bashful orchids along the fenceline could be induced to reveal
a blossom or two if only supplied with a little wet encouragement?

Was there a message hidden somewhere by a lazy robin that
yes, we could use a few more night-crawlers stretched out on
the driveway this morning? That the salamanders were anxious
to spend a few sunless moments out in the open? That the
spiders needed yet another reason to run for cover in the corners
of the garage? That the children wanted real mud between their
toes?

Dash those notions, for a moment at least, romantic clods.

"Leaf expansion in many plants requires moist conditions,"

said UW-Madison plant ecologist Tom Givnisch, though he noted that, current optimistic observations aside, instant (as in overnight) sprouting is not likely.

"When the trees are droughted, they produce hormones that retard expansion of the bud and leaf, and encourage root growth," he said.

"But when it rains, it promotes leaf expansion," he said.

"And they feel less stress."

Aha.

More rain. More leaves. More shade. Less stress.

Thank you. We needed that. ■ **May 10, 1990**

Don't Walk; Don't Park; Don't . . .

I have a confession: During frequent visits to the Saturday Farmers' Market my family and I have used the bathrooms in the state Capitol Building and, while there, we have used toilet paper.

The Capitol Police have been videotaping market-goers for evidence of double parking and—here's the real crime—WALKING ON THE GRASS. They also were concerned that people who use the Capitol Square also USE UP TOILET PAPER in the Capitol building's restrooms.

Having your picture taken under these circumstances provides evidence of the heavy workload faced by Capitol Police.

I urge all Madison market-goers to this Saturday bring along their video cameras and videotape the Capitol Police doing all the interesting stuff that they do. Also, BYOTP (Bring Your Own Toilet Paper).

This just in: Capitol Police are investigating reports of people parking cars in parking ramps. Videotapes show conclusively that several motorists drove vehicles into public parking areas and then PARKED.

"It was crazy," said a security supervisor.

"They just drove in and parked, right between the yellow lines. I've never seen such wanton use of a public facility in all my life."

Videotape at 11.

(Oh yes, imagine the videotapes if people DIDN'T use the Capitol restrooms.)   ■ **August 24, 1989**

Did it Rain By You? It Didn't Rain By Us

We were ready.

We've been waiting for this. Give us your best shot, we said, laughing, hah, hah, in the face of rainfall.

Then, another dry pie in the face.

Here it comes, the forecasters said, watch out.

So we piled up the lawn chairs in the corner of the deck. We moved the petunia boxes from the railing. We put the sandbox equipment—six trucks and a road grader (never played with) and an old tea strainer (always fought for)—in the garage.

We made little dams at the corner of the sloped flower bed, so the good dirt wouldn't wash away in the deluge.

The driveway sealer bucket filled with bird feed was securely closed. Wet seed grows.

We closed the little four-holed vent thing on the top of the ersatz Weber grill. We stood in the middle of the road in front of our house, watching the clouds above the hills for the hoary shafts that mean rain.

We listened to the Brewers game with that blip-blip-blip in the background and with radio personalities breaking in occasionally with radar reports.

Here it comes, watch out, they said. I should have remembered that last Friday someone predicted that "we're in for a drought-buster today."

We looked for the extra batteries for the flashlights (in the remote-controlled race car, of course). Then we looked for the flashlights.

The kids got baths early. Family legend has it that if you are sitting in the bathtub during a thunderstorm, lightning will seek you out and they'll find you, not only dead but naked, too.

East-facing windows were closed to a crack. After two books and a homemade fairy tale, the boys were in their bunks, the five-year-old dropping stuffed dinosaurs onto the two-year-old's head.

We fell asleep Wednesday night watching Katharine Hepburn tell Barbara Walters that if she were a tree, she hoped she wasn't an elm.

Over the humid night, I sweat more than it rained six miles south of Madison.

On Thursday morning, A met B in the hallway:

A: Get enny rain?

B: A tenth, maybe.

A: Paper said a half-inch.

B: Wasn't much at my place.

C (passing by): Mine either. A thirteenth in the back yard.

A: Who got a half-inch?

B: Beats me. ■ May 26, 1989

The Heritage of Leinenkugel

A summer night, a case of Leinie's in a wastebasket filled filled with ice, a porch balcony seat in the lengthening shade.

What ho, Leinie's? Joining the company that makes Miller Lite, the George Bush of beer?

For many of us, that was precisely why we bought Leinie's. Because it wasn't made or owned by Miller, or Anheuser-Busch, or Heileman's.

And we bought it, of course, because it was cheap and because it tasted good and because it was made up in Chippewa Falls, where there are still a couple of Leinenkugels in the phone book, one named "Jake."

As a student, a bottle of Leinie's or Huber and a handful of Red Bag Cheetos was my Saturday night dinner.

If you lived on or near Mifflin Street in the early 1970s, you could buy Leinie's by the bottle at the Mifflin Street Community Co-op, for 17 cents plus 3 cents deposit.

Some of the frat boys brought back Coors from their ski trips, but we apartment guys always had a case—usually empty—of Leinie's lying around, being used as a stool or a coffee table or bookshelf.

It was a great feeling knowing you were drinking beer that, with the name Leinenkugel, just had to be the real thing. Will the label now read "A Division of Miller Brewing Co." instead of the simple "Brewed and Filled by Jacob Leinenkugel Brewing Co. Chippewa Falls, Wis."?

Instead of promoting the beer that is "Brewed with Pure Spring Water," will we start seeing commercials along the "Tastes Great—Less Filling" line? How about something like a "Can't Spell It—Can Too" debate?

Even today, a case of Leinie's returnables costs only $5.99. And if you are really bursting with nostalgia, you would buy that case at Steve's Liquor on University Avenue. For many years, Steve's was the only place in Madison you could buy Leinen-kugel's beer.

"I'd say it was a couple of years after I opened, probably 35 years ago, that I brought in Leinie's," remembered Steve Varese, who still runs the liquor store on University Avenue.

"I was a conductor on the railroad, the Milwaukee Road, at the time, and I also brought in the old Mineral Point beer (Mineral Springs beer, long gone now) to Madison and sold a ton of that, too," he said.

"The fellow named in the paper, who sold the company, used

to come in here all the time," said Varese.

So, J. William Leinenkugel, great grandson of Jacob, used to stop in Madison to see how his beer was doing?

"Yep, he used to stop by, then his boy started going to the university here and his boy would buy beer here all the time. When he had parties, I had to get him barrels of it," Varese said.

In those days, 25 cases a week is what Steve would sell and that "was moving pretty good."

In 1972, I would guess that on Mifflin Street alone 25 cases of Leinie's was a slow week. (A person who answered the phone at the Co-op Thursday said they don't even sell Leinie's anymore.) Anyway, Leinie's is going to the big guys at Miller and I don't like it one bit, no matter how many promises the vice presidents of corporate affairs make about preserving "the tremendous heritage associated with Leinenkugel."

The point is that for Miller, Leinie's is already being called a "specialty beer." That's where the change will be. It was an ordinary beer, now it's a specialty beer. I can already taste the difference.   ■ December 4, 1987

The Arrival of Summer Daze

he heat follows me, sticks to my cuffs. Standing alone on an asphalt parking lot is like being at the bottom of a funnel of heat. Sunglasses left on the dashboard burn the bridge of my nose.

An unrelenting heat has rearranged the stage for the summer of 1988.

I get up an hour earlier than usual—5:30 a.m.—so that I can sit on the back porch to drink coffee and read the paper. By 6:30 a.m., the porch is too hot for comfort.

Because of the heat, I leave for work earlier than usual and I notice that a lot of others join me. It is cool in the office.

I wonder what section of the lawn needs watering today. What section did I water last night? Is the garden hose long enough to reach the front yard? Will the new sugar maple tree survive if I water it every day? Should I really be worrying about all this? Or should I worry three months from now?

It is the discomfort. It is knowing that a morning shower is not enough, that the walk from the parking lot to the office will leave me wringing with sweat and smelling like someone I wouldn't want to share a cab with.

And it is knowing that, without a hat or sunglasses, I risk baking my forehead, causing permanent eye damage, or at least blistering my ears.

It is shedding any formal clothes in favor of the loose, the casual, the light, only to need a sweater in the air-conditioned office. It is noting the irony of catching a cold during a heat wave.

It is hot feet, even hot breath, not only mine but everyone else's.

This heats means adding countless small weather-related tasks to the daily routine.

Such tasks as learning how to aim the water sprinkler, remembering to close the curtains and pull the shades before leaving the house, to fill the ice-trays, to pick up one of those cardboard sun deflectors for the car windshield.

The day continues and I worry. I worry about the long-haired cat being left outside too long (it isn't), about the car overheating (it doesn't), about wearing socks that are too thick (they are).

I wonder why the library seems to be so busy, then remember that a library is an air-conditioned room open to the public.

I put a big cooler in the trunk of the car to take along to the grocery store so that the perishables do not perish on the way home.

It is an atmospheric insult to even boil water, so it's salad for dinner. A glass of water on the side because I have been drinking too much diet soda pop.

The baby can go without a diaper for a while. It's too hot for plastic pants. No one leaves the house without a hat and sunblock.

Inspecting outside after dinner, I notice the insects that coat the undersides of the perennials. With no rain to provide a natural cleaning, the driveway is all dust. The candles left on the porch railing have melted into globs of wax. An angry red heat rash has begun to take over my neck and narrow lines of black dust form in the wet wrinkles of my wrist.

All of the day's clothes go in the hamper. The basement TV room is an easy place to linger and read with the TV off, in the moist coolness.

In bed, I listen for the air conditioner to click on, shudder to a stop, click on again. It is cool, but I cannot sleep. I am already thinking about the next day's weather.

It's the heat, that's what it is. And everything that goes with it.

■ **June 26, 1988**

On the Road in Search of Good Junk

I stomp on the accelerator and my newly tuned 1984 Toyota roars on to Fish Hatchery Road, going from 10 to 12 mph in a scant four seconds.

It's lunch break and I need it. A lousy day inside, the computer system is down again. I say to heck with it, I'm going to the junkyard.

I turn on the radio at the intersection of Fish Hatchery and Wingra, a lonesome spot now that the cop who usually hides out around the corner on Wingra apparently has been reassigned.

Down Park Street past the old guys sunning themselves on a bench, past the check-cashing place that, no matter how spiffy the sign, seems just a little sleazy and out of place, past the medical buildings at Park and Regent.

Up Park Street on to campus, slowing to let the students walk across, on to Langdon and Park streets, where a genius finally put in stop signs all around. Unfortunately, there is still the left turn on to Observatory Drive, an intersection where the city's blindest pedestrians ignore the city's most obnoxious bicyclists and both the blind and the obnoxious ignore the motorists, who ignore the Spree drivers.

Wind up and around Observatory, where unsmiling students stand talking about safe sex, on past King Hall, also known as the Soils Building, where a new roof not nearly as attractive as the old is being installed.

Past Babcock, where it must be three years since they started building a rock garden and they're still at it. I see the tennis courts there have new surfaces.

On the road to Picnic Point, where my friend Norm lost his virginity in 1969, past the warrens of Eagle Heights, the landing place for all sofas, bookcases and high chairs sold at garage sales on Madison's West Side. Some trees are starting to blush, I can see the autumn arrive, but I'm not in the mood for those kinds of adjectives.

Cruise through Shorewood Hills, checking my collar to make sure the points are buttoned down. I think it is fitting that Shorewood—fairly or unfairly called a tax haven—would have a street called Tally Ho Lane.

Out Locust Drive behind Kohl's in the Shorewood Foot Hills and back on to University Avenue with a quick stop for a couple cheeseburgers at the McDonald's next to the white elephant, which some still call the DNR Building and others call the Pyare Square Building.

Past the Hill Farms Office Building parking lot, from which we watched the Shorewood Hills Volunteer Fire Department fireworks display at the last Fourth. (Seemed shorter this year, don't you think?)

Still on University Avenue up to Highway Q, where the Middleton Chamber of Commerce sign that says "Welcome To Middleton" is placed in such a way that it appears to be welcoming motorists to the Country Kitchen.

In Middleton, a blonde woman driving a white Buick convertible cuts in from a side street, oblivious, talking on a mobile telephone, probably closing a deal on a cardboard-walled condo, calculating her 7 percent, but I could be wrong.

Finally, on to Highway 12 and past Porky's Motel, which is

actually a nice place that opened long before those asinine movies of the same name.

Out past what 20 years ago was Dolly's restaurant—known to Willy Streeters as "Dolly's West"—and by Don's Mobile Manor.

First right turn takes me over a hill and into the parking lot of Schmidt's Auto Salvage.

Whenever I park here, I wonder if my car is going to be there when I get back.

I grab a screwdriver, an adjustable wrench and a needlenose pliers, stop in the shack to make sure the import wrecks are still in the corner, and point my square-toed post office-issue shoes up the dusty road that leads to trunkless Toyotas, doorless Datsuns and smashed Subarus.

I lean against a Honda which leans back. Peeking into a trunk, I find three empty bullet casings from a .357 magnum. I pull a flattened non-expense account cheeseburger from my pocket, toss the wrapping in the trunk and go on my way, jingling the shiny shell casings, chewing on the cold burger and thinking maybe it isn't such a bad day after all.   ■ **October 22, 1989**

Junkyard Stroll Takes Seamy Detour

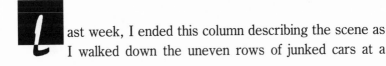 **L**ast week, I ended this column describing the scene as I walked down the uneven rows of junked cars at a

salvage yard outside of Middleton.

I had taken a drive just to clear my head and ended up at the salvage yard, wandering through the imported cars corner. As I walked along eating a cold cheeseburger, I was actually starting to feel a little better about a day that had started out lousy.

The story didn't end there . . .

Nosing through a line of wrecked vans, I see some papers through the window of a red rusty Dodge van that has been customized in a private sort of way.

I reach around through the front passenger door and unlatch the double side door to the van, which opens stiffly. Stepping in, I find I am knee-deep in unused, adult-sized disposable diapers.

There's other stuff, too. Stuff that makes me want to leave, but not before I am sure of what I am seeing.

The carpeted back of the van is covered with papers, books, photographs and photograph albums.

The photos are mostly out of focus, but a few show an adult male dressed up as a baby, wearing a diaper, carrying a baby bottle.

A couple of large photograph albums are filled with pictures of little boys cut out of catalogs and advertisements and placed in the albums in montages.

There are newsletters and pamphlets from something called "Project Truth," and a publication described as "A magazine for lovers and admirers of boys."

There is a journal from Nambla, the "North American Man Boy Love Association," which advocates sex between men and boys.

There is more, but I don't want to see or read any more of it.

I back out of the van, close the doors and write down a description and the license number.

I abandon my search for old Subaru parts and drive back to the office. I wash my hands and decide to report to police what I had found. Nothing I had seen appeared to be illegal, but I had too many questions about the van to forget about it.

County detectives later made an inventory of the van's contents, which also included dozens of reference articles about pedophilia, infantilism and coprophilia, which is a word to describe people who get sexual pleasure from excrement.

And county detectives traced the van's registration to a former UW-Madison student who just happened to be sitting in jail in California, Mo., on charges of child abuse and possession of child pornography.

It turned out Madison police detectives, specialists in such personal crimes as sexual assault and child abuse, were already looking into the van owner's Madison contacts.

And, it turned out, the FBI in Madison was also investigating the van owner's Madison activities, including his work as a baby sitter.

Madison police and the FBI have been interviewing those contacts and have so far found one complaint.

After I wrote a news story about the man last week, police were contacted by several parents who had employed the man. Officers now have a list of child-care centers that may have employed him, some of them by using references through the university, and police are following those leads, so far without finding any complaints about his treatment of children.

Steven Reinstra, a Madison detective, said the investigation of a complaint from a mother in February 1987 was stalled because the child could not provide any details of what happened. The mother in that incident called me this week to say her son, now five, is still traumatized by whatever it was that happened.

The van I found, it turned out, had been mistakenly towed to the junkyard before police could search it. It has played only a small part in what now appears to be a continuing investigation that has carried over to three or more states. The photographs found in the van were odd, but not pornographic. There were no photographs of identifiable children. The literature was a little strong for me, but by itself probably not pornographic.

As Craig Reis, a sheriff's department detective said, "It's interesting stuff from a crime-and-deviance investigation point of view, but it's not illegal."

But John Kay, the prosecutor in California, Mo., where that van owner was arrested on Labor Day as he took photographs of a four-year-old boy in the back of another van, had another point of view:

"You know, consenting adults is one part, regardless of how strange you want to get," he said.

"But the other part, involving young children, that is where this thing crosses the line, where someone starts trying to carry out these fantasies," he said.　　　　■ **October 29, 1989**

Kids' Help Brings Grins and Snickers

hat children see and hear everything is no surprise to any parent who has heard his pre-schooler blurt, "Pass the damn salt" at the dinner table.

Sometimes, though, the memory of a child can be valuable, especially when combined with that special optimism found only in the young, the sort of optimism that assumes everything is going to turn out all right in the end.

On the last day of February, Lou Madden took her two-year-old cat Snickers to the vet at the Animal Hospital of Verona for what she calls a "traumatic" exam and some shots.

"I didn't have a cat carrier or anything, so we just wrapped her in a blanket. On the way back to the car, she just jumped out of my arms and took off," said Madden.

"We (Madden and her two-year-old daughter, and a friend) ran back to the clinic. The staff came out with food and whipped cream to help find her, but Snickers was long gone."

The search was catless.

In a small community like Verona, though, Madden figured children see everything, so she went to the Sugar Creek Elementary School and got permission to put up a sign on the lunchroom door.

The sign said Snickers (who has a twin, named Milky Way, named by Madden's daughters), was lost on Feb. 28 near the animal hospital, and that Snickers was a raccoon-looking feline with long brown hair.

Madden and her daughters also put up signs at a frozen custard shop, a grocery store and the post office and took out an ad in the local weekly.

"For two weeks we went to Verona twice a day, armed with a box of cat food. We would park the car and walk around the neighborhoods looking for Snickers," said Madden.

(So the mystery of the woman wandering the streets of Verona at night, rattling a box of cat food, is solved.)

"It was like looking for a needle in a haystack," she said.

At times like this, parents tend to say one thing and think the opposite. Especially if it concerns a missing pet.

"My seven-year-old, Jaime, was heartbroken, not too sure about finding Snickers, but my two-year-old, Haley, was positive we would," she said.

She got four telephone calls:

The first was about a dead cat (not Snickers) in the road. The next was about a live stray cat, which was not Snickers, and the third was about a lady who had a live, strange cat in her attic, but that was not Snickers.

On March 12, Mary Ketterer, a teacher's aide at the elementary school, called.

A cat had been hanging around the house for two days. She had seen the sign at the school where she teaches, but had forgotten about it until her daughters, Kristina and Amanda, remembered. They were the ones who said the cat must be Snickers.

Said Ketterer: "I walked down the road calling, 'Here kitty, here Snickers' and I heard a faint little 'mew' and I knew that must be Snickers."

She lured the cat to the garage and called Madden.

"We came with a blanket and more food and, of course, it was Snickers," said Madden.

The cat, healthy, cold and "not real happy to see me," admitted Madden, was found three miles east of the clinic.

The Maddens wrote a thank-you note to Sugar Creek Elementary School, where the kids had already made a big sign that said "Snickers is home with her family."

And Jaime Madden made a picture for the children at Sugar Creek.

"She drew a picture of a family with a cat and a rainbow. It was a real happy picture," said Madden.

■ **April 10, 1990**

Still Trolling for Bargains into the Night

t was twilight Saturday and the wolves were circling the wagons in Mount Horeb.

Many had been there, on the quiet side street south of the Main Street through trolltown, since 10:30 a.m. They did not watch while the household goods were sold from wagons. Instead, they scoured the four old haywagons that were pulled into a row and piled with every kind of tool and hand-held implement, nail, bolt, wire and screw. This old Norwegian had saved everything.

It was junk and it was not junk. At auctions every weekend, men, young and old, hover around these types of wagons and pick through the boxes. They lift into the air and examine closely and at a distance an object of undefinable use, inexplicable heritage and undeniable handiness.

They take mental note of a shovel that might be useful, an extension cord that would make life easier, a set of files, a part to a long-neglected piece of machinery. Or they see something they had the match to, once, but which is now broken and needs replacing.

Or they see something and they say: "Wouldn't mind having one of those, whatever the damn thing is."

Sometimes, they stuff what they want into the bottom of a box and wait, and hope no one else sees it.

On this morning last Saturday morning, there was something on those wagons for everyone.

There was enough to convince some people to leave early in the day and return later, just to place bids on the items they remembered were on those wagons.

But this was an auction too big for its bidders. At 2:30 p.m., the wagons were still buckled under the weight of their offerings and the auctioneer was just finishing the bidding for 24 violins, one at a time (including the one with a full-length nude Marilyn Monroe on the back), which sold for as little as $50 and as much as $250.

One bidder stayed until 3:30 p.m., hoping the wagons would be next, but the sales were slow, so he left.

But he returned at 7 p.m., just as dark began to settle like coal dust over the auction. There were still three wagons left untouched, at least by the auctioneer.

Those wagons had been touched by others, though. Some items, visible and ready to buy at 3:30 p.m., were missing at 7 p.m. A fishing pole was gone, but not sold. Small items, the type of thing that would lure a bidder to a box just knowing the item was there, were missing or moved, especially from the last wagon in the row.

Men crowded around the first of three wagons in the failing light. By then, some of them had been hanging around all day. Some were muttering about the slowness of the sale, the paucity of organization. Why not two auctioneers going at the same time? No one was ready to bid any big money on anything.

The wagon loads were sold in a hurry. Men crowded to be in the first row as the auctioneer announced that the bid for choice of boxes was $5.

"$5 any box, take your pick. Howmanyawant?"

The men in the first row grabbed their boxes, shouted their identification numbers and then grabbed again, careful to slide the right box.

"$4 any box, take your pick."

More sliding of cardboard, of wooden boxes, of piles of things. It was dark now. No one could see what really was in those boxes.

The last wagon was approached.

The bidder who had returned, only to find most of what he was interested in missing from those last two wagons, had been watching the unfolding scene. A woman complained to an auction helper that she had been waiting all day and it looked like a large cardboard box of sea shells on that last wagon would be the last thing sold.

In the dark, the helper handed the sea shells to the woman and said, "Go ahead, they're yours," and off she went, sea shells clacking.

The bidder watching all this joined the chaos, at $2 a box, from the third and final wagon, where men stood along the sides, elbows moving in and out grabbing boxes, like hungry fish feeding in an ever-darkening pool.

■ September 26, 1989

Vending Machines, Like Life, A Game of Hurdles

While catching up with the local gossip in my hometown over Easter weekend, I drank six cans of Diet Pepsi, three cans of Budweiser and smoked too many cigarettes.

So many, in fact, that at one point my cousin Harry and I decided to buy a pack and split it. Needing quarters for the machine, we asked the pretty-faced, gum-snapping Rambo-ette behind the bar for change.

As she handed Harry the quarters she carefully checked each one's date.

"I'm lookin' for '74s," she said.

Are they valuable?

"Nope," she said. "They don't work in the machine."

As the evening blurred on, in between comments about ex-classmates, pregnant classmates, divorced classmates, dead classmates and classmates who never amounted to anything, I kept wondering about those 1974 quarters.

I had one in my pocket and tried it in the machine and, sure enough, it went right through and came back. Didn't work.

Back in Madison this week, an expert was consulted.

"About those 1974 quarters," said Hal Blotner, of Dane County Vending.

"We don't have anything official from the mint or anything,

but the story goes that the 1974 quarters were just a little bit thicker than other quarters, and unless certain adjustments are made on the coin accepter unit, the coin won't be accepted.

"It has not been a major problem," said Blotner.

Are there any other coins that vending machines are likely to reject?

"The only other problem we have is with Canadian coins," said Blotner.

"They don't have the same electrical characteristics," he said.

"There's a little more steel in the mixture, and they will stick to the magnets. That's why we post those little signs about Canadian coins on the machines," he said.

The rejection of Canadian coins "has nothing to do with the rate of exchange, which fluctuates wildly," said Blotner.

"Vending machine companies along the USA-side of the Canadian border sometimes have problems with banks that will not accept or give full value for the coins, but that is not a major problem here," he said.

Do vending companies find a lot of valuable coins in the machines?

"Not very many," Blotner said.

"Occasionally we will get a call from someone who inadvertently put a valuable coin in a machine and wants to get it back," he said.

"We will go out and take the cash and look for the coin, sometimes we find it, sometimes we don't."

Back to the topic of coin-detecting. What's in a vending machine that can sort out good coins from slugs and fakes and '74 quarters?

First, said Blotner, the machines have a unit that examines a coin for metal content. This is done by the coin passing between two magnets. The magnets set up an electrical field, and in passing through that field the unit checks for conductivity. That determines what sort of metal is in the coin. That's why "coin facsimiles," slugs made of brass or copper or just steel don't make it through.

Coins are also checked for hardness.

A coin inserted into a vending machine passes down a rail and hits an inclined metal rail. When it hits that rail, it bounces. It must bounce over a small hurdle and then into the proper slot. If it doesn't make the hurdle, it is returned.

As if being checked for electrical conductivity and being forced to jump hurdles were not enough, the coins are also checked for diameter and thickness. (Remember the '74 quarter?) The rails and channels the coin passes through are adjustable to allow just the right sized coin to get through.

So, a coin passing through a vending machine is a sort of pilgrim, passing through life.

If it selects, or is selected, for the right route, then there is a reward. A can of soda and a bag of chips, perhaps.

If it makes that hurdle, fine. If it slams into that rail, one of life's hurdles, and doesn't bounce high enough, it's back into circulation to try again.

Who knows, another pocket, another cafeteria, it could have been different. That night at the factory, under the flourescent lights. . .

In dealing with the vending machine of life, there's a little bit of the 1974 quarter in all of us. ■ **April, 1985**

Maybe He Should Have Left His Gum On the Bedpost

Wad's new?

Consider this evidence that truth is always stranger than fiction, from Page 1 of last week's edition of the Crawford County *Independent-Kickapoo Scout:*

"Doug Heisz, son of Ed and Sue Heisz, of rural Soldiers Grove, wishes he'd left his wad of chewing gum on the bedpost. He didn't, and he is recovering from a serious infection as a result.

"It all started when he forgot to take out his gum before going to bed one night recently. He awoke the next morning to find the gum was stuck in one eyebrow. He pulled it out but half of his eyebrow hairs came with it. It hurt, but he believed it would soon feel better.

"He turned out to be wrong. By next day it hurt more and in a couple more days the area had swelled and he had a major infection. His doctor lanced it, treated it with antibiotics and told his mother to check his temperature to make sure the infection wasn't getting any worse. If his temperature had gone up, he would have to go to the hospital.

"Luckily he showed steady improvement and although his eye was swelled shut the next day, his temperature was down.

"Because of that wad of gum, he missed a day and a half of

school, a wrestling match and some practices, and it will take six months for his eyebrow to grow back.

"You better believe, the next time his mother reminds Doug to get rid of his gum before going to bed, he'll do it."

The father, Ed Heisz, said the boy had been warned by his mother several times to spit out his gum before he went to bed.

He said the boy is doing fine now, though the wound from the lancing has not fully healed.

He also said it was bubble gum, though he wasn't sure what flavor.

Now, about that other boy who was making a face when it froze . . .   ■ **December 12, 1989**

The Seductive, Tempting Wiles of Ladies Smith, Beretta

P etite, smooth, tightly packaged, a real Lady, a temptation seductively arranged on a fluffy blue pillow. Only $235.

"Notice how it's made for a lady's hand. It's quite a deterrent, I think. And we can work a little on that price," said the mom-looking woman behind the folding table.

Hmmm. Sure feels nice. Sorry. I was looking, now that you mention deterrent, for something larger. Thanks anyway.

The woman smiled a "you're welcome" and I wandered away, reminding my son to keep his hands in his pockets as we inspected row upon row of cloth-covered tables crowded with every manner of slug-propelling instrument.

This was a gun show, sponsored by the Wisconsin Gun Collectors Association, and though we were early, we still had to park in the ditch in front of the Holiday Inn South East. The show occupied two large conference rooms across from the swimming pool.

A sign on the door to the motel bar warned patrons that no guns were allowed in the bar.

A sign on the wall in the exhibit room warned patrons that soon, no guns would be allowed, period, unless patriotic Wisconsinites gather at the state Capitol today to "support our right to keep and bear arms. Show respect for our American flag. Enlist in the war against drugs."

This rally is being pushed by Robert Thompson, a legislator from Poynette who also is a gun collector and is described as "heroic" in Wisconsin Pro-Gun Movement literature.

At infrequent intervals, a voice would squeak through a sound system in the conference rooms, urging people to attend the rally and talk to the local National Rifle Association gun-runner. The crowd may have been sympathetic, but the majority was clearly more interested in the collectibles. It might have been a flea market in Anytown, with pleasant-looking women doing needlepoint behind their exhibits of semi-automatics.

Oh, there were the camouflaged few (sweet irony, that those wearing camouflage were the most obvious) and the usual crackpots (the one booth in poor taste, I thought, was one I have seen before, at flea markets, featuring mostly Nazi memorabilia.) And how about that black T-shirt that pictured a revolver pointed directly at the viewer, beneath the printed statement "I don't dial 911."

The image of a gun collector as some wacko hoarding AK-47s in a bunker is an incorrect one, as this gun show made obvious. Mostly, these are people who collect, repair, buy and sell guns, handguns, shotguns, rifles and ammunition, the same way book collectors collect, repair, buy and sell books, paperbacks and bookshelves.

But sometimes you have to wonder if today's "guns" aren't giving gun collectors a bad name.

I could have bought an Uzi 9mm for $1,150. An Uzi is a submachine gun.

Something smaller? How about an Uzi pistol, $895?

A Chinese-made AK-47 similar to one you could have bought in Madison a year ago for $315 is now on sale for $759.

I admit I was attracted to the .22 caliber Lady Beretta because it looked nice. It certainly was no deterrent, though. And it was prettier than the Lady Smith, a .38 caliber, shiny but plump purse special for $310.

And speaking of enlisting in the drug war, how about, as a parting shot, buying what is called the "Street Sweeper"? This was an ugly, cheap-looking gun that was described as a "12-gauge revolver." Its claim was that it shoots 12 rounds of 12-gauge shotgun shells in three seconds.

Sometimes, I wonder what side of the drug war these guys are enlisting on.   ■ **November 7, 1989**

"I Can't Believe They Sold a Gun to that Guy."

Ron Bambrough went back to his workplace Tuesday and one of the first things he said to his co-workers was: "I can't believe they sold a gun to that guy."

The next morning, Wednesday, he opened the newspaper and "that guy" turned out to be an unescorted resident of the local mental health institute, confined—if that is the proper word—since 1982 while being held for a 1974 murder of a Waukesha County car dealer.

Bambrough read that "that guy," Paul J. Rasmussen, bought a gun, attacked a cab driver, stole the cab and caused four accidents and downtown havoc in a chase with police. The taxi he was driving eventually stopped itself by crashing into a utility pole in the 500 block of West Johnson Street.

Bambrough entered this story as an observer at about 11 a.m. Tuesday, when he stopped at Herman's World of Sporting Goods, 6670 Odana Road.

"I stopped in to see if they had a spotting scope, which is sort of a telescope used for hunting," Bambrough said.

Rasmussen was already at the counter and had picked out a 12-gauge Remington shotgun.

"He had already filled out the paperwork and the gun was in a cardboard box on the counter," said Bambrough.

The "paperwork" was the standard disclosure form required for firearm purchases. Rasmussen signed his real name, but he also signed a disclaimer saying he had never been judged "mentally defective."

Bambrough heard the clerk ask Rasmussen if he wanted a case for the gun, and Rasmussen said he didn't need one.

"But then he said he wanted to buy 'five boxes of ammo'."

"There were a couple things I thought strange. The man was very nervous and he had his wallet out and open. I was standing right behind him, and I don't make a practice of looking into other people's wallets, but he had an extremely large amount of bills in there," said Bambrough.

(It turns out Rasmussen had emptied his bank account that morning and was carrying more than $1,000 cash. He paid $272 for the shotgun.) Then, according to Bambrough, Rasmussen told the clerk he was a "beginning hunter," wanted to hunt pheasants, and asked for a recommendation on "ammo."

At this point, red flags started going up in Bambrough's mind.

"I'm a hunter," said Bambrough. "And I know pheasant hunting season has been over with for months. And I couldn't believe someone would want to buy five boxes of 'ammo.' And, you know, I don't know anyone who calls it 'ammo,' either.

"I just had a bad feeling. The whole thing made me extremely nervous. There was another customer about 10 feet away and I told him, 'If this guy buys a gun I'm getting the hell out of the store.'"

Bambrough left, and driving down Odana Road he caught sight of Rasmussen again, standing on the sidewalk at a stoplight.

"He had the gun in the box on the sidewalk with this bag of ammunition on top of it. He was looking up and down the street, probably looking for a bus."

Bambrough said: "The reason I'm calling is that I buy guns. I am a hunter. I don't necessarily agree with the gun laws, but this place should have exercised some common sense. I noticed this guy, how he was, and I wasn't even there for the whole transaction.

"It made me so nervous.

"When he asked for five boxes of 'ammo,' his hands were shaking. I thought he was oddly dressed, he was wearing a hat with ear flaps down and a knee-length coat.

"I thought he was really strange.

"I can't believe they sold that guy a gun."

■ March 10, 1989

Odds Are the Odds Aren't That Bad

"**I** am not a prophet of doom," said Larry Bumpass.

Yet his statistics, which turned into headlines last weekend, had more than one couple figuring their odds of survival.

And that is the very nature of his business. Bumpass, a UW-Madison professor, spends his time figuring the odds of the survival of marriages. A summary of an article for a demographics journal by Bumpass and graduate student Teresa Castro is the latest of related studies to hit what researchers call the "lay press."

The headlines said "Most marriages end up on the rocks" and "2 of 3 Marriages Fail."

Does that mean those of us still holding on to our marriages should pack it in? Are the odds that much against us? Is my marriage doomed to "fail," or, as Bumpass puts it, "disrupt."

That, says Bumpass, is not what he means at all.

The study says, "Our estimate is that most recent rates imply that about two-thirds of all first marriages will end in separation within 30 years."

That is only for recent marriages, Bumpass said. And it is also only if certain conditions present when the surveys were made continue to exist.

Bumpass, who has been fielding more than 20 calls daily this past week because of publicity about the study, said he "thought it was quite sensational treatment of what is really a modest change in what was known all along: that in the last 10 years or more the risk of marital failure for recently married couples was on the order of 50 percent. We are saying that number is higher."

The facts are that 50 percent of marriages end in divorce and an estimated 6 percent end in separation without divorce. That adds up to 56 percent, but according to Bumpass, this number should be stretched to at least "two-thirds," which is a big jump.

This only appears to be a major league waffle, said Bumpass.

The 56 percent is simply a number "on the way to another number," he said, noting the figure is pushed to two-thirds because of so many unreported separations and divorces.

Why unreported, or why don't they show up in the surveys?

Divorced people might be more reluctant to be interviewed,

said Bumpass, or might not want talk about it if it was a painful experience, or, in the case of men, may not want to tell anyone they have been divorced because they are withholding child support.

Back to the prophet of doom.

This image of a marriage ending in "failure" is bothersome, though, and it was this perspective I wanted to hear about from Bumpass.

It seems to me that if a marriage lasts 19 years, then ends in divorce, to call it a "failure" ignores what may have been 18 years of success.

So what's the matter with saying, instead of "2 of 3 Marriages Fail," that "2 of 3 potential divorces are successful?"

And since when is a marriage successful just because it continues?

Is marriage like a Rolls Royce, which never breaks down, merely fails to proceed?

"I am disinclined to use 'doomed' or other harsh words to describe how marriages end," said Bumpass.

"This is because the divorce may represent an improvement in life's circumstances," he said, emphasizing "may."

He also noted the "downsides" of that, especially the proven financial impact on the children and usually women in a "disrupted" marriage.

So you think these types of statistics don't matter?

It is the nature of things to compare, and people are always comparing their lots to the lots of others, especially in marriages and relationships. "Am I normal?" and "Does this happen to other people, too?" are familiar questions.

These statistics are important for the social changes they reflect, even predict.

Family roles are changing and will continue to change, and the likelihood of divorce has steadily increased. The length of this trend, say Bumpass and Castro, suggests that current trends of "marital instability" are "not just a response to recent changes in other domains such as fertility, sex-role attitudes, female employment or divorce laws."

What's coming? The sociologists point to increasing individualism (me, me, me first, and women saying it, too). At the same time, it has never been more clear, the study says, that divorce is "a case where the interests of children and adults in the family are often very different."

And, Bumpass and Castro end with what may be a more important suggestion than the headline-grabbing "disruption rates."

Instead of being concerned about "restoring a nostalgic family of the past," perhaps social policies should be aimed at solving the financial burdens of women and children in single-parent families.   ∎ March 19, 1989

His Cup Runneth Over

Don't take this wrong, dear, but would you like another cup of coffee?

So a Michigan study shows men and women who are regular

coffee drinkers are much more likely to be sexually active than people who aren't. Researchers are puzzled by the survey, but it shouldn't really surprise anyone. The aphrodisiac qualities of coffee have been a well-kept secret for years. I hate to see it made public, though.

I suppose now there will be a movement to ban coffee cups in public places.

Coffee shops will be zoned out of existence, or at least limited to locations more than two blocks from elementary schools. Protesters will picket in front of Victor's and Steep 'n' Brew on State Street and anti-coffee guerrillas will spray paint gratuitous slogans on walls in the wee hours of the morning.

Stores will be raided by vice cops looking for such sexual paraphernalia as coffee cups and coffee filters. Delicatessens that deliver will be taxed as escort services.

Mr. Coffee will come out with an X-rated video with the Boys from Brazil. Linda Ellerbee will come out with a poster.

Java will become one of the words banned from radio.

Uptight families will keep their coffee equipment "collection" locked in a cabinet in the corner of the closet. Sociology departments at Big Ten universities will hold colloquiums, inviting Juan Valdez and his donkey to share their insights on the personal fulfillment of coffee bean picking. High school kids will keep coffee filters rolled up in their wallets and purses.

Coffee klatches will meet in abandoned warehouses. Geraldo will do a special on "safe coffee" or people who take their coffee without sex.

Someone who says "perk up" will be sued for sexual harassment. Coffee cake magazines will replace cheesecake and beefcake. There will be tiny advertisements in the back of trendy magazines soliciting "SWFNBD" or "Single White Female Nordic Blend Drinker."

Sports Illustrated will come out with a special spring issue of people sipping, smelling, stirring, pouring but not actually drinking coffee.

Planned Parenthood will start a birth control campaign under the slogan "Wake Up and Don't Smell the Coffee."

Tables will disappear from in front of sofas in living rooms all across the Bible Belt.

And then, the networks will present a docudrama, starring Mrs. Olson and Joe Dimaggio and their lovable son, Juan, and how they survive Juan's sexual awakening at brunch with the football coach's wife. Of course the coffee drinking will only be simulated.   ■ January 20, 1990

A Prom is Sorry Note: You Be Judge

I have never stood up a date.

I have canceled a few, mostly due to work.

But I have never just not showed up.

I have been stood up—the worst being on my birthday in 1972, not that I remember any details about that clear night, temperature about 25, I was wearing brown cords—so I can understand part of what is going through Tomontra Mangrum's mind.

Tomontra, 15, goes to school in West Palm Beach, Fla. She had a date for the Palm Beach Lakes High School prom with junior Marlon Shadd.

He stood her up, she says.

Now, she is suing him for $49.53, according to an Associated Press story.

That covers her non-returnable shoes ($26), her hairdo ($23) and a flower for her hair (53 cents). She was able to return the $280 dress.

The prom was set for April 7. She talked to Marlon on April 2 and, she says, he said he had already rented his tuxedo and bought the tickets and was rarin' to go.

The night of the prom, he didn't show and she waited and waited and in the end, her mother tried to find him, but couldn't.

The boy, a basketball star, claims he told her he had broken his ankle and couldn't make the prom. He also met with a college basketball recruiter out of town that night.

The boy's mother offered to pay the girl the money, but apparently Tomontra (or her mother) wants the boy punished.

The judge says he is taking the case seriously, trying to decide whether there was a valid contract.

If she wins this one, I wonder what will happen to all those "I have to wash my hair that night" excuses high school boys have been hearing for years as girls tried to weasel out of dates. At least the girls usually gave excuses. The boys simply didn't show up.

I still ask my wife out for a date once in a while. The difference in going to a movie now, though, compared with when we were dating, is that we make a date to see a movie because we want to see the movie.

When we were dating, I would have gone to anything, just to be in the same place with her.

Also, when I was in high school, I made dates with the baby sitter and our date was to baby-sit.

Now, I need a baby sitter to make a date with my wife.

Sometimes, we end up baby-sitting anyway.

When I met my wife, we were working at the same restaurant in Oslo. We saved our tip money and went out to eat once a month. Married people, I assumed, went out to eat all the time.

Now, a big night for us is eating at a restaurant that doesn't keep a pile of child booster seats in the corner.

Anyway, back to the present, to sue someone for not showing up for the prom is about as basic a lawsuit as you can get. Isn't breaking a promise the basis for most disputes?

Side One: You promised to take me to the prom. You didn't show. You owe me for the hairdo, not to mention the embarrassment. Simple as that.

Side Two: But, I called and canceled. Besides, the last time I asked you out, you said you had to wash your hair that night, and I saw you at the mall anyway, with dirty hair.

The Judge: Never mind all that. These things are quickly forgotten. Let's talk about what happened to me on my birthday in 1972.

Which is the long-road way of saying I'm on neither side of this case.

You have to wonder about a parent who urges a teen-ager to file a lawsuit rather than try to learn something from an experience, especially after the other side offered to reimburse the money.

And you have to wonder about a kid who would leave a date in the dark on prom night.　　　　　　■ **May 18, 1989**

The Real Attractions on Train Riders are In the Cars

I got a post card from my wife the other day. She and the boys are visiting her parents in Norway. She said our two-year-old, Eivind, liked his first train ride so much that now he cries whenever he sees a train leaving without him.

I know how he feels.

For a while there, I wondered if I could catch a train at all.

The plan was this: I would help a friend drive from Madison to Seattle non-stop, catch the Seattle to San Francisco Coast Starlight train, stay with an old college roommate in San Francisco for a couple of days, then take the California Zephyr back to Wisconsin, arriving on a Friday.

From Montana, I called Amtrak to reserve a seat. I was told I could have a seat in my dreams, if I liked, but not on the sold-out Coast Starlight.

I called from Coeur d'Alene, Idaho, with no luck.

I tried a different tactic, immediately dialing Amtrak after hanging up. Presto. Seats available. All aboard.

So that's what I was doing for about a week, riding trains and learning a few more things about people who ride trains, people not in a hurry, for financial or personal reasons—to get anywhere.

I eavesdropped my way to California on what Amtrak employees call the "Stress Train."

Two young mothers sat in front of me, talking about tattoos.

Mother A had just acquired a rose and unicorn tattoo. She bared her shoulder to Mother B, and the talk turned to the least (breast and butt) and most (ankle) painful places on a body for a tattoo.

Across the aisle sat two living anachronisms, innocents from the 1960s, smelling of canned crab meat. The couple, ages about 40, sprawled over four seats. Flower Mom started a chat with Mother A about breast feeding. Flower Mom's acquaintance slept and, when awake, looked angry.

Later, Flower Mom told me she has three children and was on her way to Mexico with her Angry Man, whom she met on a train last year. Flower Mom was a fan of author Paul Theroux, probably the best living writer about trains, and we talked about our favorite Theroux books until the Angry Man awoke and demanded attentions.

Amtrak has destroyed the little ambiance that remained in its sleazy lounge cars by installing television sets and playing videocassette movies. The result is passengers cannot relax with a drink and stare out the windows at night.

The lounge car is filled with kids watching *Police Academy V.*

I like to stare into the darkness. I even look out the windows when the train goes through tunnels.

Behind me sat a couple from Hawaii. They said the Islands are still giggling about the University of Hawaii football team's victory over Wisconsin last year.

After a couple of days roaming around San Francisco—I've been there before, but this time Fisherman's Wharf looked a lot like downtown Wisconsin Dells—I took the Wednesday noon Zephyr east out of Oakland. (Amtrak does not really go to San

Francisco, it only goes to Oakland and passengers go by bus to San Francisco.) It wasn't until Reno that a fellow, an 82-year-old New York deputy county treasurer, sat next to me. He now raises burros in Richmond, Va. We agreed that if the train got any more behind schedule, we would suggest they change the lounge movie from *Wall Street* to *The Great Train Robbery.*

Behind us, occupying six seats, was a family of seven, with one on the way. They ate only the food they brought with them in coolers. (Try that on a Northwest flight to Seattle.) The kids, aged eight months to about eight years, were quiet and they all slept like dead pigs at night.

Once, when the fatigued Mom returned from the restroom, her little girl made the day by announcing: "Mom, you look brand-new."

In front of me sat a woman from England, and her two children. She lives in St. Louis, and was now on her way home after visiting 14 states by train and taking 600 photographs. She was defiant in announcing this total.

"I even took pictures in North Dakota," she said, though she couldn't remember what she took pictures of.

An inventor sat in a booth in the lower lounge, dazzling children and trying to interest people in his invention, which was a sophisticated version of Tinker Toys.

The attendant used to work the Chicago-to-New Orleans train that Amtrak employees call the "Chicken Bone," known by everyone else as the City of New Orleans. It's called the "Chicken Bone," she said, because most of the passengers bring their own food, usually fried chicken.

The Zephyr rolled into Chicago about 90 minutes late. The only casualty along the way was a three-year-old boy left unattended by his parents. He fell from an upper sleeping berth and got a nasty head cut.

This train was a village for two days only. There was gossip galore, accidents, fumble-giggle-beneath-the-blankets trysts, a couple of drunks, a fellow who played the flute in the smoking section, a mysterious, cool, unattached blond woman, a thuggish fellow in a "Rooster Booster" T-shirt, an 11-year-old girl who couldn't stop talking loudly about her parents' divorce, the Oakland Babe Ruth League All Star baseball team, and a family of mom, dad, two sons and one daughter, all perfect, apparently ordered from Sears.

None of the trains I was on departed or arrived on time.

I got to the Milwaukee Badger Bus depot at 8:02 p.m.

The bus had already left at 8 p.m. On time. Back to the real world.   ■ **August 7, 1988**

George R. Hesselberg, a columnist for *The Wisconsin State Journal*, attended classes and graduated from Bangor (Wis.) High School, UW-Madison and the University of Oslo, Norway.

He has co-written one unpublished novel, *Cocktails at Molotov's or The Plaid Thermometer*.

He has worked as a cheesemaker, signpainter, peanut-brittle salesman, studded snow-tire changer, bartender, Norwegian telephone company nightwatchman, artist's model, tin roofer, stage crewman, gravedigger, farm laborer, truck driver and translator. He collects umbrellas and knows two auctioneers, Richard and Eldon, by their first names.

John Kovalic is a syndicated cartoonist and a writer for *The Wisconsin State Journal*. He befriended George Hesselberg because George was the only person he know who would lend him money.